"I think there is a good story here. I don't know what impressed me more: the unusual things about Sasha or the extent of CJ's love for her? CJ is an animal lover extraordinaire. *Sasha, Extraordinary Dachshund* kept my interest all the way through and touched me, which is what any author hopes to do with readers."

— *Tim Woodward,*
award-winning journalist for
The Idaho Statesman and author

"Even those who aren't pet lovers will find redeeming value in this charming and poignant tribute to a remarkable dog named Sasha. The author captures the joy and pain of being owned by a little dog. I recommend this book for anyone who still believes in the strength of love and treasures memories of that favorite pet."

— *Elaine Ambrose, award-winning*
author of Menopause Sucks.

"This is a story that will touch any pet owner's heart. CJ Adams has managed to tell the reader of the incredible bond that occurs between a pet and owner. For anyone who has ever had that special pet, this message rings so true. Each chapter so resonated with me and reminded me of the wonderful, unique pets that I've owned. The emotions are real – from joy to despair and everything in-between. Sasha reminded me so much the special dogs I've had in my life and moments we had together that will forever be cherished. A beautiful, heartfelt story of love!"

— *Jayne Black, Jayne Black Consulting*

"As a devoted animal lover, I adored this book. I feel like I missed out by never having met Sasha. She was a very special character, with an "old soul" and exceptional perception. The roller coaster from paralysis, to medical miracle and then the end - the ultimate kindness and heartbreak touched my heart at every twist and turn."

— *CJ Verhalen-Ensign, US Bank*

LJ Adams
2/25/15

Sasha,

Extraordinary Dachshund:

A Memoir

CJ Adams

Dachsie Love
Boise, ID 83714
www.dachsielove.com
3rd Edition

ISBN: 978-0692379622 (Printed Version)

Photography by Barbara Johncox, Boise, ID
Cover art by Jeff Jenkins, J Jenkins Design, Boise, ID

Printed in the United States of America on post-consumer recycled paper

Preface

The Human Animal Bond will never cease to amaze me. In veterinary school, it was a buzzword that I often heard but didn't fully comprehend as a young acceptee into the program at Washington State University. An elderly, respected veterinarian, Dr. Leo Bustad, gave after-hours seminars to the students about "The Bond." I had some faint image of a person who could not be physically separated from the small fluffy dog in their lap. My first year of practice in Yakima, Washington was basically a no-appointment necessary, no money needed, free for all mixed animal practice that taught me how to think fast and be calm but it still did not illuminate the depth of the concept.

It wasn't until I started to practice veterinary medicine in Boise, Idaho that I began to understand the impact and full meaning of "The Bond." A large beautiful woman, recently married, began to see me for her rat's care. Rats have basically been genetically engineered to be experimental tumor factories and most rats will eventually die of cancer. After three surgeries that bought her beloved rat, Daisy, an extra year (comparable to 30 human years), she came into the practice for humane euthanasia, crying and sobbing. At her request I first sedated Daisy and then I carefully administered the lethal drugs into the abdomen for humane relief of her pain.

When I pronounced Daisy deceased, a low moan came from the owner's mouth and surprisingly lasted for ten minutes. I hugged and cried with her till she calmed down. Even more surprising, she then produced a beautiful piece of white beaded satin and lace and requested I cremate the scarred, cancer ridden frail rat's body in the shroud she made from her own wedding dress.

I was so touched by that experience I began to see my life's purpose, my whole reason for existing, and the direction my career needed to move towards. I was born to ease animal suffering and to be the family veterinarian for life; to help both humans and animals from that first six-week old puppy counseling exam to that end-of-life home euthanasia visit. My pet patients know my voice, my smell, my touch and I began to see that I could be their "Vet For Life." I discovered these pets bit less, wagged their tail when they entered my parking lot or building and trusted me to help their pain.

I will always remember that extraordinary beautiful red dachshund named Sasha who always recognized my voice and rewarded my possibly terrible day with a happy tail-wag and lots of kisses. To see her in the prime of her life, through her painful back ordeal and then to be there for her at the sunset of her life with blind, white eyes yet still with that trusting tail-wag, is my whole reason for being. I get up in the morning every day because I know I have in my hands, the power to help decrease the pain and suffering of both the pet and the family. Sasha taught me about the Human Animal Bond... and I will never forget her.

Dr. Dawn Sessions, DVM

Prologue - Why was Sasha Extraordinary?

"Get OFF the table!" I yelled at Sasha. It was not like her to ignore her manners when we had guests but Sasha would not move or even acknowledge that I yelled at her. Sasha had her own mind and she could be defiant when determined to get at something she wanted, but this was not the situation. Sasha was standing on top of our kitchen table with her nose less than an inch away from Susan's lips. Susan was frozen, not in fear, in fact she had no idea Sasha was there. Susan was experiencing an epileptic seizure that caused her to zone out, her eyes wide open but she was completely unaware of anything.

Susan's seizures could last from 20 seconds up to two minutes and I had witnessed them a few years earlier when she visited with us in Modesto, California. At that initial introduction, Susan, a delightful, pretty, young lady who was engaged to Mel's cousin's son had several similar seizures while enjoying dinner with us. They were not like any epileptic seizures I had either heard of or experienced before. You could only tell she was in a seizure because her eyes opened really wide and she sat perfectly still. The family explained that the seizures are referred to as 'absence seizures' and that Susan also experienced them while standing and walking and often fell but didn't actually go into convulsions.

Sasha was about three-years-old when Mel's cousins surprised us at our front door in Boise, Idaho. They had purchased a small RV, and were taking a family trip around the Pacific Northwest. They remembered we had moved up to Boise and decided to look us up. Mel and I were on our way out the door for nine holes of golf so we left our surprise guests to visit with Polly, Mel's mother. When we returned later that evening, Polly was very excited because they had invited her to join them on their trip to Yellowstone National Park. She made arrangements for them to pick her up early the next morning.

I made a pot of coffee and some cinnamon rolls for us to enjoy before they left that morning. Mel was helping to load the RV with Polly's things while the ladies sat around drinking coffee. Sasha was always excited to have guests, you see, as she firmly believed all guests came to our home with the explicit desire to shower her with affection and compliments. Sasha had always been so well behaved and as long as she was in someone's lap she was content to remain there. I was standing in front of the oven, which was inset into an island/counter top that separated the kitchen from the dining room. Polly was seated at one end of the table with Sasha in her lap. This was not normal, Sasha did not sit in anyone's lap while we were at the table but she had refused to stay down because she knew those suitcases being carried out the back door meant Polly was leaving.

Completely out of character and quicker than Polly could react, Sasha jumped on top of the table and bolted across stopping just at Susan's face. Startled, Polly spilled her cup of coffee and, everyone else at the table jumped up as I yelled at Sasha. I pulled the cinnamon rolls out of the oven then threw a hand towel toward Polly to wipe up the spill. While we were all reacting Sasha just stood there, tilting her head side to side, as if studying Susan. Sasha should have bolted away from all that commotion, especially knowing she was in trouble, but she just stood there staring at Susan. Dachshunds are not pointers but Sasha appeared to be pointing at Susan. Her little legs were on the very edge of the table as she was leaning toward Susan with her tail perfectly straight and level with her back.

I made it around the counter to help clean up the coffee spill, everyone had calmed down and Sasha was still less than an inch from Susan's face. I was transfixed watching Sasha perfectly still and was going through the motions to remove her from the table top in slow motion. Suddenly, as quickly as Susan had entered her seizure, she came out of it. She was surprised to see a red dachshund staring into her face so she leaned back a bit and said, "Oh hi there little one." I was standing there with my arms out to get Sasha when with her front paws, Sasha inched her way up Susan's chest and snuggled her head on Susan's left shoulder. Susan tilted her head toward our affectionate dachshund and Sasha reached up with her left paw and stroked Susan's cheek. Susan immediately scooped Sasha off the table and cuddled her in very close. The two of them connected in a way no one else could understand while the rest of us just looked on in amazement.

Sasha would not leave Susan's lap and that was just fine with Susan and I was not about to get in the middle of what they had going on. They carried on their own little conversation for about 20 minutes while the rest of us enjoyed our coffee and cinnamon rolls. Naturally, our entire conversation centered on Sasha's actions.

Our cousins informed me that some people with epilepsy had service pets that were trained to warn their owners of an impending seizure in time for them to get to a safe place. This was all very fascinating, but more important it was the incident that made me realize Sasha truly was extraordinary. It was not my imagination or biased feelings toward her that made it so; it was her actions with other people that confirmed it for me.

I had to physically retrieve Sasha from Susan's lap when it was time for them to leave. Susan mentioned she would look into service pets when they returned home because of that experience. She had been told of service animals but now she knew it was possible for her. Another species was capable of empathizing and that could change her quality of life. When they returned a week later to bring Polly home Sasha and Susan were best buds during their hour-long visit. Susan did not experience another seizure but Sasha was stuck to her like glue and I think she thought it was her job to watch over Susan.

Our cousins offered to buy Sasha as I retrieved her from Susan's arms, but there was no amount of money I would have accepted. Sasha was mine. She may have been able to understand or even predict an epileptic seizure, but she had an even greater gift. Sasha spoke to my soul.

"When I die, I want to come back as CJ's pet."

Mel Adams

Mel and CJ

I met Mel when he applied for a job as a warehouseman at the company where I worked as the controller. The decision to hire for this position was given to the sales manager and me as the previous three people hired by our general manager had stayed on the job less than a month. The part-time position Mel applied for did not pay well and he was way over-qualified for it. We would have been thrilled to have someone of his caliber in that position but we knew he would eventually leave us for greener pastures.

During this same time period my mother, LaWanda, and I joined a bowling league. We were new bowlers but thought joining a league together would be fun.

Sasha, Extraordinary Dachshund

Much to my surprise I ran into Mel at the bowling center. He recognized me and came over to chat while we bowled. I liked this handsome man, we could laugh easily together and Mom was taken with him as well. A few weeks later one of our team members didn't show up for league so I asked Mel if he would be a substitute bowler on our team. This upset our opponents for the evening. Mom and I were the only ones at that bowling center who were clueless about Mel's bowling abilities.

It turned out Mel used to bowl professionally and our team was good-naturedly taunting us for bringing in a "ringer." Mel was as humble about his abilities as he was impressive in executing them. He was poetry in motion (and still is) when he's throwing a 16-pound sphere 17+ MPH on a 60' long lane with deadeye aim at ten 3lb-6oz pins. I was later informed by his scratch league teammates that Mel's nickname was Mr. 300. (At that time he had bowled eight perfect 300 games.)

Me? I trip over paint lines. There was no poetry in any of my movements. Even though Mel had taught many people to bowl it was beyond his considerable skills to make me a better bowler. Over time we became good friends and I realized this was the man I could spend the rest of my life with. About a year after meeting Mel I asked him to marry me – he said no. It took me six hours to convince him to say yes but he finally did. And that story could be another book so I will not go into details in this one. Suffice it to say at 25-years-old I, till death do us part, married my 38-year-old soul mate.

I admit that I am the eccentric one in our relationship – we both have our quirks...I just have more than my fair share. Mel is always at an even keel, good, bad, indifferent – he is always the same and that can be comforting. I, on the other hand, am all over the place but no matter what direction I am moving in I always have and will return to my center, Mel.

Mel and I moved to Idaho from San Jose, California in October 1993. We left California with everything we had in a U-Haul truck. Because we had nothing lined up for housing we knew we would move into an apartment, which probably wouldn't accept animals. Prior to that move we had Blondie, a beautiful and very spoiled cocker spaniel. It broke my heart to give her up because Wes, my stepfather, gave her to me as a puppy for Christmas 1991. I had never been given a puppy as a gift before. Even though Wes knew Mel would not be thrilled with this puppy he knew it was the best gift for me. After struggling with the fact I had to give Blondie away, I interviewed several prospective new families. I chose a retired, widowed lady who needed a beautiful animal to love. It turns out she had always had cocker spaniels, prior to the sickness and death of her husband, and she instantly fell in love with Blondie. I felt at peace knowing my Blondie would be spoiled and loved by her new owner as much as she was with me.

I cannot recall a time in my life that I did not have a pet, either a cat or a dog. I always had an animal to care for and love. Any stray, any breed and just about every temperament, I loved them all. I smile now when I think back on all the strays I 'found' or 'who followed me home' and at how my family accepted each one. The look on my father's face seemed to say, "I can't deny she is my daughter because she looks like me, but where did this pet obsession come from?" Growing up, we moved many times so I was familiar with the heartbreak of giving up a pet and my parents did their best to make it as easy as possible on me. When I gave away Blondie, I knew the time would come for me to find the perfect pet, I just didn't know this particular pet would be extraordinary.

Mel knew I loved all animals; in fact, I had three cats when we married in September 1987. With his wry sense of humor Mel would tease me saying,

"You know, you're supposed to wait until you are an elderly eccentric widow before you start collecting cats?"

Blondie required monthly grooming and because we had a mobile groomer come to our house each month, it was expensive keeping our Cocker spaniel looking great, to say nothing of the vet bills for teeth cleaning, vaccinations and general care. I've always taken excellent care of my pets. Mel knew that particular aspect of me owning a pet would never change but he thought if we got a dog that didn't require constant grooming then maybe it would not be so expensive. He chose a dachshund as the perfect, low maintenance, therefore inexpensive, dog for us to love.

Mel's story: In his own words -

I was at a picnic in Modesto, California celebrating our team winning the state-bowling tournament. It was 1979 and a team member arrived at the picnic and told us another one of our team member's dog was delivering puppies a bit early. He explained the dachshund bitch was having a difficult

time so this team member would not be celebrating our victory with us. After the picnic I decided to go over to check on my friend and his animals. The bitch delivered five pups but died giving birth to the last one. Other friends happened to show up and in that sad moment we all agreed to take the newborn pups to raise. I was 30-years-old and never had a pet before much less a puppy. I just got caught up in the moment and offered to help.

My family traveled the picking circuit between Oklahoma and California every year. In fact, I was born in a converted chicken coop in Florence, Arizona while they were trying to get to Oklahoma because Dad wanted me to be born in Coolidge. Our lifestyle did not allow for a pet, sometimes we barely had enough food for ourselves so feeding a pet was out of the question.

This newborn pup was quite a sight. He looked just like a bald mouse and could fit in the palm of my hand. His dad was a Chihuahua and his mom a dachshund and he was only an hour or so old. I took him home and made a bed for him from a small shoebox and put it under a lamp for heat. I called a local pet store and some friends for advice on what and how to feed this pup. I learned he would have to be fed every two hours with an eyedropper. Fortunately I had a job in which I could keep the pup with me all the time. I was his mother and I kept to a strict routine of feeding and cleaning him.

After about three weeks of constant care he started looking like a puppy, his ears were standing straight up like he wanted to hear everything going on. He was still very small and his ears seemed to grow faster than everything else. I was a big Star Trek fan and thought of Mr. Spock every time I looked at this pup so that became his name. Spock was always with me and it was strange caring for something constantly but we bonded. I had never experienced this kind of bond or affection before. Spock was as devoted to me as I was to him. He was so smart and as he grew I taught him tricks. I didn't know how to properly train him but whatever I did it worked. Spock was quick to learn everything. We became best friends and it was cool to have something be so devoted and trusting toward me.

I taught Spock to sit up so I could place a little hot dog on top of his nose. He would sit there staring at that piece of hot dog and just wait for me to say, "Get it." Then he'd tilt his head sideways and snatch the piece in one swift move. Of course, I thought this was too cool so I would make him sit there longer and longer before giving him the 'get it' command. I guess one day I took it too far because he just gave up and dropped the snack on the floor. He looked up at me with an expression that said, "Just give me the treat and stop playing around with me." What a smart dog! I was hooked and loved him like nothing else.

Life gets in the way and unfortunately due to job changes and an impending move out of state, I had to leave Spock with my Mom. Mom had never had a pet either but she agreed to watch him for 'a little while' but wanted to make sure I understood this wasn't a permanent thing. I left Spock with her while looking for a new place and came home to get him a few days later. I found a place I could keep him and wanted to take him with me. Mom refused to let me have him back. She explained that Spock was at home there and she didn't want to upset him again by moving. Of course, I could visit whenever I wanted. I still laugh at these thoughts. Mom had never wanted a pet but she wasn't about to give up Spock.

When Mel and I arrived in Boise, we rented an apartment and started house hunting. We purchased a home with four bedrooms, two bathrooms and two stories built in 1949. It required major renovations and we wanted to restore it. We moved in during the Christmas holidays of 1993. The home sat on just under a quarter acre and was surrounded by chain link fence. Now we had a home and yard that was perfect for a pet. So as my 32nd birthday present we drove to Emmett, Idaho to look at a litter of dachshunds.

Before I tell you all about Sasha let me give you some personal history of pets and me. When I think back about being raised the middle child of a Southern Baptist Minister I remember our family life always revolved around the church. We moved a lot; as a very young child we moved so Dad could complete his education and as an older child we moved because Dad was called to minister to different churches. I believe my love and bond with animals was my way coping with the changes. I never had trouble with moving from state to state or to a new city; in fact, I learned to look forward to the moves. The only time a particular move was traumatic for me was when I had to leave a cherished pet behind.

I can best describe my family's view of pets like this: Dad tolerated them, Mom loved them, Mark and Carrie enjoyed them and I bonded with each one. I knew Mom loved all the critters I came home with and to this day I think that co-love of my pets was the beginning of our friendship. She is my Mother, and I am grateful for that but more importantly she is my best friend and that is one of my life's blessings.

I requested my parents tell the stories they remember of my animal devotion while growing up. Their words are bold and are what they wrote. I added my comments in regular font.

From my Mother – LaWanda J. Richardson

The first pet I remember having was a stray dog that came with the old farmhouse we were renting in Dothan, Alabama. CJ was about three years old and she followed that old dog wherever it went. It let her hug it, ride it, sit on it, whatever, without any problems. Unfortunately, a car hit it just a little bit before we moved. CJ went around looking for that dog and was so sad when she couldn't find it. She couldn't understand it was dead, all she knew is she didn't have her playmate.

That same year we moved to Hattiesburg,

Mississippi for her father to attend William Carey Bible College. It was the first time that we had lived in a big city. We lived on a street with lots of people and lots of kids. One of our neighbors down the street had a large dog, I don't remember what kind it was (a beautiful German Shepherd) *but anyway all the kids were in our yard playing and CJ went up to hug the dog, like she had done to ours previously. Well, guess this dog didn't like hugs as he bit her on the face, just missing her eye.* I was eating a peanut butter sandwich and this dog was trying to take his own bite of the sandwich but got my face instead. *We had to take her to the emergency room.* I had stitches next to my eye and mouth. I was only five-years-old and determined not to cry because I didn't want anyone to think a bad dog bit me. *That was the third time that dog had bitten someone so after keeping it under surveillance for ten days to check for rabies the owners had it put down.* I was devastated at this. The dog just wanted a bite of my sandwich and I begged everyone to please not kill it because it was not his fault. I was unable to understand I was the third person bitten. I remember not wanting to go outside to play for days.

Later she 'found' a kitten. It was snow white so we named her Snowball. CJ carried her around like a baby. And of course you know she slept with CJ. She also was later run over by a car. I had a little funeral and read from the Bible, just as my father did. My brother Mark put Snowball in her grave and my sister Carrie put flowers on her and we buried her properly. I cried my eyes out for several days. This would be the first of many funerals we had for my animals. Mark, two years older and Carrie, eighteen months younger than me always understood and never made fun of me.

The next pet we had was a stray cat. We were again living out in the country of Clara, Mississippi when this big, wild tomcat started coming up to the house. None of us could touch it but after starting to put some table scraps out, it got to where it would come up and rub against our legs as we were sitting on the back porch. But if we tried to pet it, it would run away. This went on for several weeks before it would finally let us pet it. So, of course, once we were able to pet it, there was no stopping the kids from trying to bring it inside the house. Guess it had never been inside a house before for as soon as they brought it in the back door it made a beeline to the front door and went flying out, busting the screen off the door! Mark, Carrie and I tore after that cat like we were scalded. It must have made for a comical sight but we knew we were in trouble. We lived in a parsonage, which is a home provided to the minister by their church. I remember my Dad was not happy but the deacons replacing the door all laughed when Mom told them what happened. *After that, one day when the kids were gone, I took the cat inside with me and he jumped up on my sewing desk, laid in my thread drawer and that was his spot whenever I was sewing. We named him Thomasina. We had him several years and right before we were to move to California he disappeared. It broke all our hearts but none as much as CJ's.* I never got to say goodbye and we never knew what happened to Thomasina. We moved back to the same church and house three years later after dad finished seminary and Mark, Carrie and I looked for Thomasina for weeks but we never found him. I was devastated for the second time, as I never got to say goodbye to Thomasina.

While we were living in Pittsburg, California, we went to visit with both of my sisters in Southern California and they each had toy poodles. The kids fell in love with them so when we got home we started looking for a poodle. We found this ad for a standard poodle so CJ and Carrie went with me to look at them. The lady was explaining how they were 'French Poodles' and that they had to have 'French' names. The father was named Bonaparte and the mother was Josephine. So the girls went off into another room and soon they were back. CJ said, "We have a French name! It's "FRENCH FRY!" I thought the lady was going to die laughing. I don't remember what we named her but we didn't have her very long. Unfortunately she died of hepatitis a few weeks later. Even though 'Frenchie' was Mom's dog, I still conducted a proper funeral for her. We believe Frenchie contracted hepatitis from another dog that was being groomed at the same time. This is the reason why I had mobile dog groomers come to my home to groom my cocker spaniels.

Later that summer we went back to visit with my family and my sister said that she had a toy poodle she would give us. She had

11

given it to her grandchildren and they weren't taking care of it. It had a broken leg. We named him Pierre. It was love at first sight! Pierre was definitely Mom's poodle. We all loved him but he was devoted to Mom the most.

Later on a church member gave us one of their pups. It was a Boston terrier mix. He was pitch black. This became CJ's dog! She named him Frisky. Or sometimes she called him Frisky Bob. He was small but very protective of the kids and me. I taught Frisky to sing with me. This drove my family and neighbors crazy, as we usually didn't sing softly – I screeched and Frisky howled. I had so much fun and Frisky was the best dog and my best friend and he was just as rambunctious as I was. *Well, having two dogs wasn't enough for CJ, no, she just happened to find a kitten "that followed me home from school!"* I believe every proper home needs a cat, don't you think so?

I don't remember that kitten's name. I named him Sammy. *I just remember that it used to take the foiled wrapped chocolate Christmas balls off the Christmas trees. I was blaming the kids for taking and eating them until I saw the cat and Pierre one day. The cat would sit on the arm of the couch and knock the chocolate ornaments off the tree and hide them behind the couch where they would both tear into them. It's a wonder it didn't kill them.* When Mom pulled the couch away from the wall, the evidence was there and we were so happy she found it because up until that time she believed we kids were lying to her.

We were in Pittsburg, California about three years when we decided to move back to Clara, Mississippi. There was no way we could take three pets with us. We found someone to take the kitten but not Frisky. He would not let anyone come close to us girls so people were afraid of him. So before we left we had to take him to the pound. It broke CJ's heart and I don't think she ever forgave us for it. This was my first experience with having to give up an animal I LOVED before a move to another state. It never became easy and I can remember the heartbreak of each departure to this very day. We were taking Pierre so I just couldn't understand why we couldn't take Frisky too.

We had Pierre while we were in Mississippi and after several years we moved to Palatka, Florida. It wasn't long until CJ 'found' another kitten. I came home swearing on the Bible to my father that it just followed me home. Dad felt bad I had to leave Frisky so he let me keep the kitten. I don't remember its name because unfortunately a stray dog killed it. *Evidently, some animal attacked this kitten as my son, Mark, found him one day and buried him before CJ could see him.* I came home from school looking for my kitten. Mark was waiting at the back door and took my hand and led me to the kitten's grave. Mark was fifteen and I was thirteen at this time. I was devastated and upset because I couldn't have a funeral. Mark was crying as he said,

"I had to bury it before you saw it, the kitten was running up a tree and the dog bit its butt off. I couldn't let you see that!"

Mark assured me he had a proper funeral but had saved the cross for me to place on the little grave. My poor kitty, what a horrible way for her to die. My family understood how much I grieved for a lost animal.

I surprised her with a new kitten she named him Snoopy. Mom surprised me with a "trip to the store" but actually took me over to a friend's home whose cat just had kittens. They were five weeks old and the friend wanted us to wait another week before getting a kitty but I just couldn't wait. I found the perfect kitten. He was solid black and just stunning. *CJ would lie on the floor to watch TV and Snoopy would curl up in the middle of her back and lay there until she got up.* I had carried him around inside my shirt until he got too big. Snoopy waited for me at the bus stop every day and even waited outside our church on Sunday mornings to walk me home. He became a very big cat and stayed with me always.

Our son Mark had a science project with tiny white mice. Every now and then one of them would get out and you would find Snoopy 'playing' with them. He never hurt them, just chased them all over.

There was a blue jay that used to come and sit on a telephone pole every day at about the same time and Snoopy would go outside and that bird would swoop down and attack him. This went on for several weeks. It was quite a show. I like to think that Snoopy got the best of that bird because one day it just disappeared.

Just before our move to Jacksonville, Florida a car killed my Pierre while we were on vacation. We had left Pierre with church members while we looked for a place to live in Jacksonville and they were devastated that this happened while they took care of him. They buried him before we returned. I was most affected by Pierre's death as we had him for many years through many transitions in our lives. We left Palatka and moved to an apartment complex in Jacksonville that did not permit animals. Again, I had to leave an animal behind so I gave Snoopy to some friends who eventually lost track of him because he'd always run away from their home back to ours.

We later got another poodle we named Cheri. After a year or so we moved to Davie, Florida taking Cheri with us. We were now all working or in school and Cheri did not seem happy. CJ had a friend who had a little sister and she would take Cheri with her when she went over there. Eventually we gave Cheri to the girl and they were both very happy.

Later, while living in Ft. Lauderdale, Florida, we got another kitten that also was run over. CJ cried for days. I had named him Bugger and he was a British Blue kitten. And like Snoopy, he was devoted to me and we were always together. I swore from that day forward I would never allow another cat of mine to live outside. *We were given an 8-month-old German shepherd puppy from a church member we named him Bandit.*

Sasha, Extraordinary Dachshund

That was the last pet she had while living at home. He was blonde, like beach sand, except for a black mask around his face. He was given as a gift to Mark, Carrie and I but he became my dog. Day and night, we were inseparable. Bandit rode around in my 1965 and 1967 Mustangs and would patiently wait in the car wherever we went.

Bandit became hysterical when it thundered and this happened a lot in South Florida. He ate the lower eighteen or so inches off the door leading from our garage into the kitchen and busted through several windows during a hurricane. We had always attributed this to some kids throwing firecrackers through our chain link fence at him on a July 4th holiday. Bandit and I had play-wrestled all the time but, completely out of character, he took an aggressive stance toward me one day. Bandit was exceptionally strong and protective and sometimes aggressive to strangers but he'd never stood up against any of us. A church member who happened to be a veterinarian agreed to examine Bandit and took x-rays that showed there was a tumor in his brain.

This tumor explained Bandit's behavior and also made him an unpredictable large dog. We had people over to our home constantly and were not willing to risk someone getting hurt. I will never forget taking Bandit to the clinic to be euthanized. I was shaking and sobbing while leading him into the room. The veterinarian would not let me stay in the room while he euthanized Bandit so I sat on the floor, outside the door and cried until I was informed he was dead. I didn't take him home because we had agreed to a necropsy for research so there was no proper funeral. I just had to pick up the pieces of my heart and go

16

home alone. I was seventeen at this time but felt like a little girl who had lost her first pet. I swore I'd never get another animal; the pain of losing them was just too much to bear.

Today, looking back at our family and my childhood years, I believe that having an animal was a coping device for my Mother, not just an indulgence for her children. She married Dad at the tender age of fifteen and had Mark, Carrie and me before she turned twenty years old. Mom was raised in Seeley, California and married Dad while he was in the Air Force stationed in El Centro.

From My Dad - David C. Edenfield

My wife and I had three children, a boy and two girls. CJ was the middle child and the animal lover in the family. It wasn't unusual for her to come home carrying a kitten or a puppy in her arms and stand in front of me and lie through her teeth and tell me it followed her home and ask could she keep it? CJ was never one to lie to me, but when it came to animals the rules changed and she would do whatever was necessary to keep the animal. She was a 'dyed in the wool' animal lover and as her daddy, being soft hearted, she always got her way.

The only time I remember her getting mad at me was when my current wife, Donna and I spent Thanksgiving 1997 with Mel and her in Boise, Idaho. We knew that CJ had Sasha for several years and at that time she was explaining to us what had happened with Sasha and how they were treating her with acupuncture. CJ and Mel had already spent a lot of money on trips to the veterinarian and I knew this was expensive, even though CJ never said anything about the expenses.

Being the realist I am I knew she'd mortgage her home to pay for treatments and, not thinking it through, I suggested she consider putting down Sasha if it happened again. Too late...I realized I had stepped over the line and broke my daughter's heart. As planned, the following day Donna and I left for home. CJ was mad at me and barely spoke to me before we left. So true, we had to drive them to the airport and I just couldn't understand why my dad could say something so heartless. He repeatedly apologized but it was said and it took a long time for me to get over it. *It was several months before I could get her to talk with me and beg her forgiveness. Never again did I mention putting down an animal to CJ.*

Dad was not an animal lover to my extreme but he appreciated the companionship they offered. He was raised in Jessup, Georgia on a farm, the youngest of nine children. To him, animals were for working or eating and they lived outside. Dad was just practical and couldn't understand how a human could spend so much money on a pet – he thought you could always just get another one. This made me realize he had never really bonded with an animal and my heart hurt for this emptiness in his life.

Mark and Carrie were also animal lovers but not as obsessive as I was. I don't recall either of them having a pet of their own as we were growing up but they always loved whatever pet lived in our home. For some reason the pets always seemed to be mine.

Mom and Dad divorced amicably in 1985 and that allowed our family to be blessed with wonderful stepparents. Mom married Wes Richardson (a fellow animal lover) in November 1991 and Dad married Donna Grebe (the perfect step-mother) in March 1996.

Sasha, Extraordinary Dachshund

CJ Adams

"There is no psychiatrist in the world like a puppy licking your face"

Ben Williams

Getting Sasha

Mel and I arrived to see this precious litter of five puppies the end of January 1994. The day was overcast and cold but the sun was shining in my heart and that was all I could see. I would live in the middle of a litter of puppies all day, every day, if I could get away with it. I love their smell! I love their clumsiness and the way they all pile on each other to sleep. I love how innocent and sweet they all are. Puppies are perfect creatures! I had never seen a dachshund puppy and was caught up in my own thoughts of what they would be like. The whole drive over I was like a kid in a candy shop.

Because we were still new to Idaho, the city of Emmett seemed a long way from Boise. Emmett was mostly rural and country roads bisecting cherry orchards in a bedroom type community of about 5,000 residents in 1994 that was only about 30 minutes from Boise. We were in the middle of an Idaho winter and driving over Freeze-out Hill caused me to gasp a few times. Once we crested the hill I loved the expansive view of farmland, pastures and orchards. This community sits on the Payette River that provides all the irrigation water to the farmers, lots of fishing and water recreation. I don't think we got lost but I remember thinking that these people live in the boonies.

We arrived at the address to find a nice farm style home with a dirt driveway and a big front yard. It was painted a nice gray and there was smoke coming from the chimney. We were invited into their lovely home and immediately felt at home. The furniture looked comfortable and was covered with blankets and quilts. We could tell this was not the home of a professional breeder, but just good dachshund loving people. To my delight I was among five adorable, six week old puppies falling all over themselves on the hardwood floors. The puppy momma was beautiful and she greeted both Mel and me from her blanket on the sofa. She was a standard size, red in color, gentle, well-mannered dachshund that was four years old. She wanted to be among her brood but was told to stay on the sofa and she did so until I begged her owner to let her down. I believe her name was Queenie and she had eyes that intrigued me and I wanted to love on her. We never saw the father but were informed he was a black and tan miniature dachshund that belonged to friends of theirs. I sat on the floor and all five puppies came wobbling over to me. It was funny because the puppies had all just gorged themselves and their bellies almost drug the ground as they romped around on their little legs just being puppies. Mel knew that I could have stayed there forever so he "encouraged" me

22

to make a decision.

Such a dilemma for me...I wanted all of them! How could I possibly choose only one? Which one is just right for me? Should I choose a boy or a girl? I'd never done this before and I wanted this moment to last a long time. I handled all of them and smelled each one but I couldn't choose just one as I loved them all, so I decided one had to choose me. I looked up at Mel and said,

"I'll lie down on the floor and the first puppy that comes up to me will be ours."

I put all the puppies by the sofa then moved over a bit to just lie there and see what happened...one female came over, attempted to jump on my face and gave me a little lick – I was GONE! She was mine and that was all there was to that. The puppy's mother came over to snuggle with me as if she was approving of this whole ordeal. This was the first puppy to be separated from the litter. I cried as Mel paid $300.00 for this little gift. I let her Mommy sniff her to say goodbye and I kissed the remaining four puppies goodbye. I believe we were walked to the car; I don't really remember the details but later Mel informed me the puppies had been given their first shots. I only had eyes for my new love. It was glorious, she smelled so sweet that I couldn't put her down.

This new puppy was mine, all mine, but on the way home I was so overcome with good feelings that I told Mel he could name her since I chose her. We had researched dachshunds and found them to be of German heritage so Mel thought a German name would be appropriate. We thought of lots of names but couldn't be sure if they were really German or not.

Sasha, Extraordinary Dachshund

Suddenly Mel said, "Sasha."

I liked it and asked, "OK, how did you choose Sasha?"

Mel replied, "Remember the Sylvester Stallone/Billy Dee Williams movie, *Nighthawks*? I think the lady in it was German and her name was Sasha, that's the only name I can think of."

Here's the funny part: the female in that movie was a terrorist who killed everyone she came in contact with. However, she was gorgeous – not sure how she smelled though. So our sweet smelling, innocent puppy, Sasha, was named after a bloodthirsty, killing machine female terrorist. I laughed at this when we pulled off the two-lane highway on the side of the road next to an orchard to let our sweet Sasha pee. It was so cute to see how small her legs were and how big her belly was as she romped around following every step Mel took. She eventually peed then immediately wanted up and in some place warm because it was cold outside. Mel gently put her into my arms and I inhaled her sweet scent. Belly full, bladder empty, it was naptime so she crawled under my sweatshirt and went to sleep for the remainder of the ride home. I was in Heaven. Sasha was the best birthday present I had ever received.

Mel asked, "How am I ever going to be able to top this gift?"

I replied, "You will never have to. Besides that, it will be impossible to top perfection."

One of my favorite things in the whole world is the smell of puppy breath and here I had my very own. Sasha smelled like all the wonderful things you can think of and she was small and adorable and mine...all mine.

Sasha, Extraordinary Dachshund

"Dogs are not our whole life, but they make our lives whole."

Roger Caras

A New Home and Family

We stopped at a pet store and promptly purchased everything necessary to make our new puppy comfortable including a purple collar with paw prints on it. Then it was on to our home to introduce Sasha to her new place. She was so tiny and I didn't ever want to put her down but Mel insisted on letting her explore her new territory. Initially we kept her in a box while we were gone then we would put her outside to pee when we came home. This worked well for potty training. Mel had this weird notion that Sasha would sleep in that same box at night. He begrudgingly gave up on that notion the first night because I couldn't sleep and had to constantly comfort our new puppy. Sasha became our bed partner and promptly claimed a spot in between Mel and me. She was a good sleeper as long as she was snuggled under the covers.

The next day I looked in the phone book for a veterinarian and found one just a few blocks from our home. Our first visit on January 31, 1994 to Broadway Veterinary Hospital was incredible. The clinic was converted from an old home located at the busy intersection of Broadway Ave and Beacon Street. The exam rooms were the bedrooms, the entrance was the living room, the surgery room was the kitchen and dining rooms and the kennels, x-rays and offices were in the basement. The entire staff had to handle our new puppy and they all sniffed her. I knew this was my kind of place; puppy sniffers – gotta love them! I met Dr. Dawn Sessions and was instantly taken in by her eyes and smile. We were the same size in height and weight and she had a deep voice like me. She smiled constantly and laughed easily. Sasha weighed 3-1/2 pounds at this first visit. Sasha was given her second shots and her toenails were clipped. Dr. Dawn encouraged me to play with Sasha's paws and ears so that she would be a good patient for the staff in the future. That was never a problem. Sasha LOVED visiting the vet's office. Dr. Dawn went over a puppy wellness plan for Sasha's first year and we religiously adhered to it.

On the second visit to Broadway Veterinary Hospital we entered through the front door and sat to wait our appointment time. The front staff immediately approached me so they could hold and sniff Sasha. After a few minutes we heard Dr. Dawn laugh while she was examining another animal. Suddenly our little Sasha howled like a big dog and I couldn't quiet her down. It was cute at first but she wouldn't quit howling and I was terribly embarrassed. Even as a puppy Sasha had an incredibly loud bark – but this was a howl that I am sure you could hear if you were standing across the street. Dr. Dawn escorted out her current patient and as soon as Sasha saw her, she went wild wagging her tail and howling.

Dr. Dawn was giving instructions to another pet owner, trying to ignore the racket in her clinic but grinning the whole time at this demand for her attention. Much to all our relief this other patient finally left so Dr. Dawn looked down, belly-laughed and pointed at Sasha's frantic tail wagging saying,

"Oh look at that happy factor! Someone is happy to see me today!"

Sasha finally quit howling because now she had Dr. Dawn's undivided attention. From then on we called Sasha's tail her "happy factor." And I am embarrassed to admit that in the fourteen years Dr. Dawn treated Sasha, she howled as soon as she heard Dr. Dawn's voice and continued to do so until she was given Dr. Dawn's undivided attention. Sasha LOVED Dr. Dawn and she was the only person who made Sasha howl.

Sasha, Extraordinary Dachshund

First Years

Sasha was too small to traverse the stairs into our home and up to our bedroom. This was never an issue, as I loved carrying her around. It was a proud day for Sasha when she finally got big enough to get up the steps on her own. This meant she could go outside by herself so we installed a doggie door into our backyard.

Sasha developed one bad habit that we were never able to break. She hated water and cold weather. She was not going to get her paws wet and certainly had no reason, in her mind, to ever be cold. During the winters she never made it out the doggie door to pee, she just relieved herself on the rug inside the house next to the back door. If it was warm outside but the grass or ground was wet, she relieved herself on the rug at the bottom of the outside stairs. We did everything over the years to break her of this habit but never succeeded.

Sasha took to the leash quite easily. However, she never learned to heel. And true to the dachshund breed, she always wanted to be in the lead. I had such a hard time pulling on her collar because it choked her, as she was determined to be in front, so I purchased a harness. She only wore the red harness on walks. She realized when I picked up the red harness it was fun time! She even learned how to step into the harness to make it easy to get on. This was one of the first occasions I witnessed her thinking about something. She taught herself to put her right leg in, then stick her head through and then slip the left leg in for me to buckle it around her chest. When I took her red harness off the coat rack hook she immediately sat down to wait for me to bring it to her level.

I initially had thoughts of breeding Sasha just once so I could experience having puppies in my home. Even though he indulged most of my desires, Mel knew this was NOT a good idea as I would NEVER be able to part with any puppy born in my house. I'm not sure if Mel secretly consulted with Dr. Dawn prior to my discussing breeding Sasha, but Dr. Dawn explained that dachshunds frequently experienced high-risk pregnancies. No need to say more, I couldn't risk something happening to Sasha so we had her spayed in March 1995.

Mel supported this decision because he remembered the mother of his first puppy, Spock, dying shortly after delivering her litter. Sasha was just as special to Mel as she was to me. My handsome Mel was 45-years-old and Spock had been the only animal in his life. Even though we'd had several animals in our combined life together I knew Mel also sensed Sasha was unusual.

"My sunshine doesn't come from the skies, it comes from the love in my dogs eyes."

Author Unknown

Always Sunshine

There was no better feeling than be greeted by Sasha at the door. You could be gone ten minutes or ten hours and it was still the same happy greeting. I'd swear her tail was going to fall off because she'd wag it so furiously. Sasha had different greetings for Mel and me. While she was just as excited to see either of us, she had different routines for us. For Mel it was: greet at gate, rush through the doggie door, dance around crazily when daddy came in, then prance prettily toward treat jar and jump around until treat was obtained. For me it was: greet at the gate, rush through the doggie door, dance around to be picked up when I came through the door, pepper my face with kisses and howl while I sang "You are my sunshine, my only sunshine," as we danced all the way to the treat jar. Regardless of the outside weather it was always sunny inside our home.

I don't ever remember being disappointed getting out of the car, entering the gate and having such a precious creature so very obviously happy that I was home. At that moment it didn't matter what had happened during my time away from home or what kind of mood I was in. It was as if I had just taken a drug when I dropped everything in my arms to pick Sasha up for a happy dance. All my other pets prior to Sasha were always happy to see me but this was different and much more intense. If only I could have bottled and sold that sunshine!

CJ Adams

Traveling

We took Sasha everywhere with us and she loved to go. She traveled well and everywhere she went people fawned over her because she was so lovable. On an eight-hour trip up to Coeur d'Alene for the state bowling tournament with some camping friends, Darrell and Mary, we stopped at a restaurant for dinner. We left Sasha in the car snuggled in her travel blanket. After our meal we came back to find bits and pieces of the two large Baby Ruths and two large Butterfingers we had purchased as traveling snacks strewn on the back seat. These candy bars were wrapped tightly in a plastic bag that was wrapped again in a paper sack and stuffed under the front passenger seat. I was angry for about half a second then was beside myself with worry because dogs shouldn't have chocolate. Poor little Sasha's belly was all swollen but she was her happy little self. Even though she was miserable for gorging on four candy bars, Sasha seemed quite proud of her foraging skills, as she had to crawl under the seat to dig through the CD's, umbrella and first aid kit to get at the loot.

I wanted to call 911 but cooler heads (Mel) prevailed

and he convinced me to call Dr. Dawn. Fortunately this was an evening Broadway Veterinary Hospital was open late so I frantically phoned for advice. The wonderful staff all had a good laugh but assured me even though the four candy bars were large they didn't have enough chocolate on them to kill her, however, she was going to get sick so be prepared. Oh, she got sick all right. All night long in our hotel room I was cleaning up her 'processed' evidence. When Sasha started to eliminate her 'loot' I'd rush her to the tub, this kept the nastiness confined to the bathroom but it was a whole lot of activity going on all night. I am not the most coordinated person to begin with and being sleepy and trying to minimize the damage to the hotel room I was not the quietest one either. My poor Mel, he was the anchor bowler on their team, hardly slept before having to bowl in the early morning time slot of the state tournament. Sasha and I slept the morning away while Mel bowled. I scoured our hotel room as we had to stay another evening and Sasha was none the worse for the experience and we all survived. Mel's team placed 2nd that year and he was in the money for the singles and doubles brackets that year. Funny thing is Sasha never wanted candy again. Imagine that!

Back Problems

In June 1995, Sasha and I were visiting my Mom in Fresno, California. Mom was living in an old farmhouse on property owned by my sister, Carrie and her husband, Greg. The house was small with only two bedrooms separated by a bathroom. I loved this old house because it was quaint and had farmhouse character and was basically out in "the sticks" of Fresno. As always, Sasha slept in bed with me and on this morning she wouldn't get out of our bed to go snuggle with Mom and me. We have always done this morning snuggle and it included our pets. Mom had her Shi Tzu, Pepper, and both of our spoiled pets were good buds. I realized Sasha hadn't followed me after I crawled in bed with Mom and Pepper so I went back into my bedroom. Sasha was sitting perfectly still in the middle of the bed, her tail not wagging and, not making any attempt to move. She was whining, not like she was in pain, but as if she was saying "Come get me, I wanna snuggle."

I picked her up, put her on the floor and softly scolded her for being such a princess and expecting to be carried everywhere. She didn't move so I thought she was just being stubborn and I walked back to get in Mom's bed. Sasha didn't follow me. I waited a moment then started to call her to come get in with us. Pepper jumped off the bed and went to Sasha then came back by herself. Sasha whines turned into soft barks. I realized something had to be wrong because Sasha never missed an opportunity to snuggle in a warm bed. I got out of Mom's warm bed to get Sasha who was still in the same spot I left her. I gasped and called for Mom,

"Come help me! Something is wrong with Sasha!"

I picked Sasha up, she didn't cry out or give me any indication something was wrong. Still barefoot and in my pajamas and needing to relieve myself, I took her outside for morning potty and went in to mine. I went back out the front door and found Sasha in the exact spot I sat her down. She made no attempt to move or pee. That is when panic set in, I started crying because I realized something was wrong with my baby and that she needed help and we were 700 miles from home and Dr. Sessions. Mom understood this was not just an animal issue, this was me, her daughter who loved this animal with all she was capable of, and she knew I would have gotten in my car and driven straight home to get help for Sasha. Being a lot more in control of her emotions that I was at that moment, Mom suggested we call her veterinarian and request an emergency appointment, which they granted us. We hurriedly dressed and off we went with me in panic mode the whole time.

The last incident of me forgetting everything in a panic and hurrying to a vet's office involved our dear cocker spaniel, Blondie, in Modesto, California. I was soaking in our hot tub just outside the sliding glass doors when I observed Blondie staggering and gagging. I jumped out of the hot tub, raced inside and saw Blondie fall over in convulsions. Without thinking, I scooped her up, grabbed my car keys and sped off to the vet's office. What a shock for the receptionist! Barefoot, dripping wet and only in my black bathing suit I rushed in carrying Blondie as I breathlessly explained what was happening and bolted into the closest exam room. Fortunately a tech came rushing in; she took Blondie from me and whisked her away into the surgery room where the doctor had just finished a procedure on another animal. It turns out Blondie's convulsing and seizing was typical of poisoning and she needed immediate care. I was oblivious to my appearance until the receptionist graciously offered me a towel to dry off with and a lab coat and some booties to wear as I waited for the diagnosis.

After much discussion we came to the conclusion Blondie must have licked the kitchen floor after Polly, Mel's mother, had sprayed under the cabinets with Raid to get rid of ants. Because of this incident we switched to natural products for insect control and read each product label very carefully to insure it was safe for our animals.

The drive into Fresno proper from Mom's home took well over twenty minutes. Mom did her best to calm me down and reassure me that all would be fine. She never belittled the love and devotion I had to my pets and she knew Sasha was different – extra special. Mom is so good at calming me and she always has just the right words to soothe my thoughts and fears so I was calm and rational by the time we met with the veterinarian.

Sasha, Extraordinary Dachshund

After a full evaluation of Sasha, in which the veterinarian would not allow me to be in the room for, the veterinarian bluntly explained that Sasha's only chance at recovery was to leave her there for three days. Have you ever entered a place and felt that something just wasn't right? The staff smiled at you but didn't really mean it? Not only was I in distress but I couldn't shake the negative vibe being thrown at Mom and me.

This veterinarian was not nice, and she certainly didn't seem to have my or Sasha's best interest at heart. I don't remember the exact conversation but by the time this pompous veterinarian finished insulting my ability to care for Sasha I was hyperventilating. Mom and I were stunned by what this veterinarian was saying and by the way she was talking to me. The shock of it made me unable to think clearly. That and the fact I was hyperventilating were the only reasons I didn't punch this woman. Mom will tell you today that she was impressed with the fact I didn't deck this woman. I wanted out of this evil place something fierce!

After I calmed a bit and could safely handle her, I took Sasha out to the car. Mom dealt with the receptionist and waited as they copied the x-rays. Out in our car I called Dr. Sessions and she advised me to come home with Sasha. I agreed to leave the next day and promised to keep Sasha confined to her crate the entire time. I don't believe Mom ever took her animals to that horrid lady again.

It is a fourteen-hour drive from Fresno to Boise and I left Fresno at 9:00am on Friday. I had Sasha in her crate seat belted into the front passenger seat. Being in her crate the whole drive must have been annoying for Sasha because she loved to look out the windows. Dr. Dawn promised to wait for me to arrive so she could personally examine Sasha. I stopped at pay phones to call Mel and assure him I was safe and not in panic mode for this long drive. I also called Dr. Sessions' office and the receptionist repeatedly assured me she would be waiting. I arrived at Broadway Veterinary Hospital around 11:00pm and Dr. Dawn was there. Think about it, 11:00pm on a Friday night. What a goddess!

The x-rays from California didn't show an "obvious L1-L2 disc collapse" as the sadistic Nazi-veterinarian had written. Dr. Dawn took another series of x-rays and still did not concur with the Fresno witch doctor's assessment. Sasha would put up with anything Dr. Dawn did to her as they had some kind of connection that was all theirs. During this examination Dr. Dawn poked and prodded all along Sasha's spine. She even squeezed Sasha's back paws with pliers and that only caused Sasha to barely respond to what should have been extremely painful. Dr. Dawn prescribed Prednisone and instructed me to keep Sasha confined and to call tomorrow for a follow up examination within three days.

I can't explain how appreciative I was of Dr. Dawn's commitment to the well-being of Sasha. It was midnight before we left the clinic. I asked that she charge me extra for her late night efforts but she flatly refused. I kept at her about what I could do to show my gratitude as we walked out to our vehicles until she finally stated, "I like Bud Light."

Sasha responded well to the medication and confinement and was her usual perky self by the follow up examination three days later. I showed up with a

12-pack of Bud Light and from that day forward, for over ten years, I took a 12-pack of Bud Light to each of my visits involving Sasha at Broadway Veterinary Hospital. The staff came to call me the 'beer lady.'

Dr. Dawn and I discussed, at length, what caused this episode and could never determine why Sasha's hind-end 'went down.' Dr. Dawn explained that some dachshunds are just prone to back issues usually caused by jumping up and off furniture or even playing with larger dogs. She recommended we discourage Sasha's furniture jumping and that we keep all other large animals away from her. Sasha recovered quickly and without lasting effects. Life was normal again.

Polly, Mel, CJ and Sasha, 1998

Sasha and Polly

Sasha continued to rule our household especially after Mel's 66-year-old mother, Polly, moved from Modesto to live with us the summer of 1995. These two were made for each other. Polly loved Sasha as much as Sasha loved her. They even had their own language. Sasha had a daytime snuggle partner and someone to take her down the road to Garfield Elementary School during recess for all the petting and admiration any animal could wish for. Polly and Sasha were a pair made in heaven and Sasha had Polly wrapped around her paw in no time at all. Polly would often say, "Sasha took me for a walk today" and she meant that.

Sasha had an agenda and knew just where to go and at what time for maximum petting and loving time. If Polly attempted to alter their walk direction Sasha would just sit down and refuse to move. This was their daily routine unless it was raining or icy outside. It wasn't a long walk and dachshunds don't walk too fast so it was perfect for Polly.

After their walk it was time for apple pieces. Each day Polly cut up half an apple to share with Sasha. Polly could get away with eating two bites to Sasha's one bite but absolutely no more than that. And Sasha wanted her apple pieces every day, no exceptions. I had the privilege of witnessing this daily event many times and it always amazed me how Sasha had complete control. I so loved that Polly went along with it and enjoyed letting Sasha be in command of their days. Sasha could only get away with this kind of behavior with Polly and she knew that and took full advantage of it.

I mentioned Polly and Sasha had their own language and I want you to know it was unique to them. Sasha barked a different tone when communicating with Polly. Sometimes it was a continuous session of small barks, almost like a sentence. Only Polly understood what Sasha was saying. Sasha 'talked' to me pretty regularly but not to the extent or in the same tone she did with Polly. A good example was bedtime. About a week after Polly moved in with us Sasha followed her to bed and they became sleeping partners from then on. Polly usually went to bed before Mel and me at around 10:00pm. Just as the news would come on the TV Sasha would extricate herself from the blanket on my lap and head straight for Polly's bed. If Polly didn't follow within ten minutes or so Sasha would come back into the living room with an obvious air of irritation and 'tell' Polly it was time for bed. It always worked. Polly would laugh at being given the 'what for' but she always went right to bed after the 'scolding' from her bed partner. Sasha only did this with Polly. When Polly was on a visit to Modesto and not at our house, Sasha just waited patiently for Mel and I to head upstairs for bed. Naturally she slept with us but she never called us to bed as she did Polly.

Sasha, Extraordinary Dachshund

Fishing – Sasha about Three years old

Mel and I took Sasha everywhere including camping and fishing. On this particular summer weekend in 1996, at CJ Strike Reservoir, Mel was up early, alone and fishing, as usual. Mel loved the early morning solitude and the stillness of the lake water as the sun rose. Sasha slept in late, snuggled in the sleeping bag with me. Our friends, Darryl and Mary, their two young children and black lab named Cocoa, started stirring around. This meant some action to investigate, so Sasha wanted to get out of the tent to check things out. I unzipped the tent for Sasha but I wanted more time to sleep. However, Mary started the bacon frying in a pan and that was all it took to coax me out of the warm sleeping bag. I crawled out of our tent and saw Mel standing at the edge of the water casting his line as far as possible. The sun was up over the horizon seeming to signal to us that this day was going to be a glorious day. Darryl was grabbing his fishing gear to join Mel, the children were entertaining the dogs and I wanted bacon.

I joined Mary in preparing our breakfast. Labs love the water and Cocoa was fetching a stick that Darryl hurled as far as possible into the lake. Cocoa would take off into the water to retrieve her prize and bring it back to the shore. Sasha wasn't about to get her feet wet so she hung out next to Mel. She'd bark as Cocoa swam in with the stick and the two of them would play with it until Darryl threw it in the lake again. Cocoa had a happy-go-lucky attitude like Sasha and even though she was bigger than Sasha she understood Sasha was the dominant dog in this pack. When the dogs were tired you could find them resting, Sasha would snuggle her body into Cocoa's belly and push her nose between Cocoa's front legs.

That morning Mel was catching small perch and made the mistake of throwing a fish to Sasha while Cocoa was swimming out after the stick. Sasha happily carried her prize to Mary and me. I was startled and took the fish away from her because I didn't want her to eat it afraid she'd get bones stuck in her throat. Oh, she was not happy about that. I threw the fish back into the water. A few minutes later, Sasha magically appeared with that fish in her mouth. Come to find out, Sasha loved fish. She didn't try to eat this small fish she just carried it around, pleased with herself and showing her fish to the children and Cocoa. I let her keep it for about ten minutes, and then took it away to throw in our trash. I scolded Mel and told him to throw the small fish back and not give Sasha anymore.

Remember, I said earlier Sasha hates water. However, she wanted another fish and realized they came from Mel who was now knee deep in the lake. Sasha stood as close to the water as possible without getting her paws wet hoping for another fish from Mel. Cocoa would come in with her stick to share but Sasha wanted none of that stick. She wanted a fish and that was all there was to that. She would bark a Mel a bit, just to remind him that she was waiting for another one. When Mel caught the next one big enough to keep he walked in a bit to latch it onto the stringer with the other fish he'd caught. Sasha witnessed this whole chain of events and since the stringer was in the water close to the shore she could see all those fish just hanging out. A wave from a passing boat caused the fish on the stringer to drift just up to the edge of the water. Sasha got as close to the stringer as possible and drug a fish by the tail with her paw toward her. She now had another fish to carry around but it was attached to the stringer so she barked at it thinking it would just disconnect itself. This caught all of our attention. Mel walked back in, scolded Sasha while he was laughing and moved the stringer out a bit in deeper water. Sasha could still see all those fish just hanging out on the stringer and was pacing back and forth on the lakeshore working out a way to get those fish. Since this is a very popular lake Sasha didn't have to wait long for another boat wave to send the fish back in her direction. This time, however, she would have to get wet if she wanted a fish. Sasha bravely walked in and grabbed a fish by the tail and pulled it toward her and voila she had another fish.

Watching this was amusing so I did nothing to stop her. Mel could hear the splashing and called for me to come get Sasha away from the fish. I gave Mel the shoulder shrug and reminded him that he was the one who started the whole thing. I removed the fish from Sasha's mouth and heartily scolded her as I laughed and then I moved the stringer deeper into the water. Mary needed help with breakfast so I left the shore but we could still see everything going on. Sasha wanted those fish in the worst way. But now she'd have to swim to get them and no way did we think she would do that. We were wrong and couldn't keep ourselves from watching what she would do next. To our amazement, she stepped into the water until it was deep enough then stuck her head under and blew air out her nose. I guess she determined the water wasn't so bad because she was obsessed with getting at those fish. Underwater she went swimming about two feet to the stringer, grabbed the first tail she could and swam back. It was hysterical! She had her fish, could stand up in the water but couldn't get the fish off the stringer. She tugged and pulled at that fish as Mel scolded her while taking the fish away. Mary and I had to stop cooking because we were laughing so hard.

Mel, being the smarter of the two, decided he'd teach her a lesson and moved the stringer out by him in waist deep water. This was about eight feet away from the shore. The water was clear so Sasha could still see the fish but more importantly she knew where the fish were. She pranced around the water line for a while cocking her head, barking and thinking about what she had to do to get one of them. Much to our surprise she swam under the water all the way to the stringer, nabbed a tail and surfaced with the fish. I thought Mel was going to fall over with astonishment and I was on the ground in a laughing fit.

What was she going to do? She had the prize but was in four feet of water. She doggie paddled around with that fish trying to get it loose. It wasn't working so she dropped that fish and went after another one hoping to pull it loose. We were laughing hysterically by now. Sasha was swimming in circles around the fish stringer. After recovering from a fit of laughter, Mel took that fish off the stringer, gave it to her and she swam back in with her prize. Oh she was so proud of herself. I let her keep the fish and she carried it around for about thirty minutes before I took it away. She never tried to eat that fish, she only wanted to play with it. Poor fish, they didn't stand a chance between Mel and Sasha! Sasha was obsessed with fish from then on.

Sasha, Extraordinary Dachshund

No Strangers

Sasha developed a magical personality. Dr. Dawn often referred to her as a perpetual three year old. Even as she aged, she kept her youthful exuberance and curiosity. Sasha lived every day believing the whole world existed to love her and we did nothing to show her otherwise. She knew no strangers and had no fear of anyone.

When out walking or in a shopping cart with me at Lowe's she greeted each person with an attitude saying "I know I'm cute and I know that you want to pet me so get to it!" With other animals, regardless of size, she put on her Queenly attitude by standing tall, puffing out her chest and straightening her tail. She always let another dog smell her first and she'd stand perfectly still, not wagging her tail, then she'd take her turn getting to know this new four-legged friend with her tail on full 'happy factor' wag.

Sasha was never submissive to other people or animals, only to Mel. In our pack Mel was alpha male and the only person to whom Sasha ever displayed submissive traits. Sasha believed she was my equal and even though she accepted behavior corrections from me she felt shameful and sorry when Mel corrected or punished her. I never understood this deference given to Mel. Sasha was my baby, we had the connection and the bond but I sometimes wondered if she could sense my love for Mel and if she saw him differently because of that love.

Squirrels

Sasha hated cold weather, but let me tell you if there was a squirrel in her yard it didn't make any difference if there was six inches of snow covering everything, she would tear out after that varmint like it was a sunny day. I know I mentioned that she was smart, but when it came to squirrels she lost her senses. Our big back yard at the Boise Avenue house was full of mature trees and therefore we had squirrels that lived there from year to year. And you know what? Squirrels are mischievous little critters. We had a pair of squirrels that would sit on top of a birdhouse we had nailed to a tree and throw things at Sasha. These squirrels went around the yard gathering stuff just to throw down at Sasha. The birdhouse always had a little stash awaiting their next bombing exercise. It was amazing to see how many times they actually nailed Sasha on the head with their bombs. It never deterred Sasha; she was determined to rid our world of those varmints. While Sasha was serious about getting rid of the squirrels I firmly believed the squirrels were having loads of fun. I could just imagine a parent squirrel dragging their progeny to the birdhouse to teach them

Sasha, Extraordinary Dachshund

how to bomb that annoying dog on the ground.

I assume it was this same pair that knew just how far down the tree they could come to taunt Sasha. They circled the tree trunk skittering around just above Sasha's reach. This could go on for hours. Sasha never gave up! Sometimes she'd crouch down behind a bush, hiding in wait for the squirrels to breach the height boundary and when they did Sasha would shoot out of the bush like a bullet. Much to her dismay she never caught one. When I heard her "I've got something treed" bark I'd go outside, make myself comfortable on our patio and just watch this exchange and get my daily dose of laughter in. This would only end when the squirrels were tired and bored or when I stomped out to the tree to retrieve Sasha and bring her inside. Yes, I had to close off the doggie door or Sasha would bolt back outside before her paws hit the floor.

Cats

Sasha hated cats!! I'm not sure why because she was never really exposed in a negative way to them, but she hated them and would probably kill one if she ever caught it. The first example of this cross species hatred came at the home of our dearest friends, Bob and Carrie Miller. The Millers just acquired a kitten they named Molly. She was an adorable yellow cutie-pie and we wanted to introduce Sasha to cats because I loved them and we were considering getting a cat to keep Sasha company. Sasha had been to the Miller's home with us many times so she was used to its unique scents. However, on this trip Sasha went berserk looking for the source of this new scent as soon as we walked into their home. Sasha found the kitten on the Miller's bed, which happened to be too tall for Sasha to jump onto.

We had barely taken off our jackets when we heard Sasha growling and barking. Down the hall the four of us went having no idea what Sasha was doing and fearing for the safety of the new kitten. Much to our dismay we found Sasha with the bed's comforter between her teeth as she was aggressively pulling it off the bed. If she couldn't get up to this new scent then she was going to bring it down to her level. Little Molly was just frozen in terror and the comforter slid off the bed. I grabbed Sasha and could barely hold onto her as she struggled to get at Molly. Carrie grabbed Molly who had no idea what was going on but knew enough to be afraid of this maniac trying to get at her.

Carrie and I walked through the hall toward the living room while struggling to get control of our animals. She was having a much easier time with little kitty, Molly, than I was because Sasha turned into a maniac. The guys, being bigger and tougher, decided to step in to take control of the introduction so Bob retrieved Molly from Carrie and Mel took possession of Sasha as she struggled and twisted to get away from any control so she could get the kitty. Slowly Mel and Bob approached each other as they spoke softly to Molly and Sasha until they were standing right next to each other. The closer they got the crazier Sasha behaved. We had never seen her this crazed before so Mel began flicking her on the head to get her attention and correct her bad behavior. Didn't even faze her.

Carefully Bob started to lift Molly toward Sasha...unexpectedly and lightning fast Sasha lurched out and took Molly's little head inside her mouth. This movement stunned Bob to the degree he let go of Molly. Mel instinctively jerked back grabbing Sasha around the mouth causing her to let go of Molly and poor Molly dropped to the floor. Let me tell you something, kittens can really move – she may have hit the ground but I think she FLEW back to the bedroom.

Sasha squirmed like a mad dog to get down from Mel's arms but he held her tightly until Carrie could run through the hall to close the bedroom door to protect Molly. Mel let Sasha down so she bolted to the bedroom door and barked incessantly, pawing at the carpet and trying to find a way in. Mel pulled her away from the door but Sasha was obsessed and didn't care that her pack leader was scolding her, she wanted that kitten and that was that!

Fortunately Molly was physically unharmed and grew into a beautiful loving cat that hated dachshunds. Sasha never forgot about Molly being behind that bedroom door and from that time forward as soon as she went into the Miller's home she bolted to the bedroom. As Molly grew she learned to hide in the shower to get away from this maniac dog trying to get at her. Sasha never gave up or quit barking when we'd visit the Millers so we just didn't take her with us when we visited.

Even as Sasha aged, she held on to her hatred of cats. We always took Sasha with us on trips to my mother's and on this occasion Mom had a cat named Hope. Sasha was there when Hope came to live with Mom and Wes as a very small kitten and would have eaten her alive if she could. This made our trips so interesting. As time went on Hope learned to remain inaccessible to the terrorist dachshund and we learned to make sure the doors were shut tight to keep Hope from harm. We visited Mom two to three times a year and Sasha never forgot that a cat lived there. It was always a mad scramble for Mom to locate Hope, shut their bedroom door, make sure it was latched securely and move out of the way before Sasha came inside. Sasha couldn't wait to get out of the car, up the steps and inside that cat infested home. She'd tear through the living room, kitchen, down the hall and meet the bedroom door head on, bark incessantly and paw under the door hoping to get at the feline beast. Hope was a bit of a daredevil because she started pawing under the door from her side of the room. It was pure mayhem – pawing, screeching and howling until one of us made it back there to pull Sasha away from the door. Hope's litter box was located in the middle bedroom down the same hall so Wes installed a gate to one side of the hall wall and secured the other side so Sasha could not move the barrier.

For a few years Hope stayed on her side of the gate and learned she was safe there. Eventually Hope became bold and would sit on her side of the barrier and torment Sasha until one of us could no longer handle the barking and put Hope back in the bedroom. I guess Hope finally decided that it wasn't enough to just torture Sasha, she wanted a face-off with her tormentor. One evening we were all sitting in the living room watching a movie with Sasha curled up asleep on the sofa under a blanket between Mel and me when Hope sneaked up to the sofa started meowing as she pawed at Sasha's blanket. Faster than a speeding bullet Sasha was out from the blanket and at Hope's face. Hope barely escaped Sasha's teeth and managed to fly into the spare bedroom and leap on top of a shelf full of framed photographs that was 7' high.

Frames and knick-knacks came falling down on top of Sasha as Hope recovered from her near-death experience. Sasha was frantically looking for a way to get on that shelf by the time we got involved in this showdown.

Wes had to capture Hope from the shelf as Mel wrangled Sasha out of the room. From that point on Sasha looked for Hope on that shelf before she tore through the house to Mom's bedroom door. After Sasha passed away, whenever we would go to Mother's, Hope would still hiss at Mel and me. I guess she still knew we were the evil ones that had brought 'The Tormentor' into her home.

Sasha, Extraordinary Dachshund

Barking and Running

Of course, dachshunds are barkers, it is what they were bred to do. My research on the breed explains they were developed to hunt and chase badgers. Have you seen how vicious badgers are? Dachshunds can be even more so. It was their job to find the badgers and bark until their master responded. Badgers live underground, which is why dachshunds have small legs with wide paws to dig them out. They have unusual nostrils and large lungs that allow them to breathe in tight spaces. They are also very alert hunters. Sasha definitely satisfied her hunting genes with our squirrels, and we were witness to many funny events. Though the breed is small, their bark is large. If you didn't know there was a dachshund barking on the other side of the door you would swear it was a German shepherd.

Sasha never barked when Mel or I came home. I don't know how she knew it was us because she could not see our vehicles. I think she could hear the different sounds vehicles make because she would bark like crazy when it wasn't us. One afternoon, Sasha was only a year or so old, Mel came home and found me passed out on the floor in the hallway upstairs. I don't remember this because I was in a migraine but after I recovered he told me that he almost broke his leg getting up the stairs to find me. Mel said the reason he rushed in the house and up the stairs was that Sasha was barking furiously when he got out of his truck. Mel explained this was the first time she sailed passed the treat jar as she ran through the house looking back at him to make sure he was following. He will tell you our little girl went up the stairs two at a time – like she was flying. This scared him because she was too small to get up the stairs that way and he knew something had to be wrong with me.

Mel could tell I was breathing and didn't appear injured so he assumed I was in a migraine so he picked me up and carried me back to our bed. Sasha was in the bed waiting when he laid me down. She wouldn't leave me alone and according to Mel she only left my side when he was in the bedroom with me. Every now and then she'd bark – just one bark and Mel would come up so she could go outside to relieve herself. My migraines could last two – four days so Mel would bring Sasha's food and water bowls up to our bedroom when he left us to drive to work.

How Sasha managed to 'fly' up our stairs is still a mystery. I never witnessed it but I guess her long body and fierce determination propelled her to get to me as quickly as possible. Dachshunds may have small legs but boy can they run fast. Their speed is amazing, in fact, I've seen Sasha keep pace with many larger dogs. Dachshunds don't have the endurance of larger dogs and can't run for long stretches but in short distances they will beat larger dogs to the finish line. Sasha didn't run around just for fun or exercise, she ran to hunt. I didn't dare let her off her lead when we went on walks. She never lost sight of her target and with her curiosity, determination and speed she could be out of sight before I knew what was going on.

Sasha, Extraordinary Dachshund

Thinker/Problem Solver

Our Sasha was also a thinker. I never found anything that mentioned the breed as being problem solvers, like Jack Russell Terriers, but our Sasha was. You couldn't keep her out of somewhere if she wanted to be there. She would look for a way around whatever obstacle you put in front of her. We were used to this as we witnessed many a time when she found a way in to a place she shouldn't be. Sasha would move items to get to where she wanted to be. If something were too high for her she'd work out a way to build a bridge from where she was to where she wanted to end up.

We had to move our kitchen table farther away from the countertops because Sasha would jump up on a chair then onto the table top then sail over to the counters. Boy, we thought we were just too smart for her but she quickly proved us wrong. I came home one afternoon to find Sasha had pushed or dragged a chair away from the table and put it next to the counters so she could get up there. These chairs did not have wheels on them so it would have been quite an effort for her to move it the eight feet necessary across the carpeted dining room floor. Being low to the ground was seldom a disadvantage to Sasha.

Sasha, Extraordinary Dachshund

Babies (The Human Kind)

As far as I recall Sasha had never seen or been near a baby before this incident sometime in the summer of 2000. A friend, Adele, who drove school bus with me, came over to show off her two-week-old baby girl. As usual my best friend, Mary, was there and we were preparing a little party for the three of us to celebrate this new little girl. Adele came into the house carrying the baby in a removable car seat with a carry handle. As soon as she entered the house Sasha went crazy jumping up on Adele. I asked Adele to set the car seat on the kitchen table and Sasha immediately jumped on a chair and up to the table. Not knowing what Sasha would do I made her get down. Remember, she never gives up.

After getting tired of making Sasha get down we all went upstairs to set the baby on the cutting table in my sewing room. It was high enough that Sasha couldn't get to it and we could sit around and enjoy each other's company. Sasha followed us up the stairs to my sewing room and did her best to get to the baby. Sasha was beside herself and started whining then howling because she couldn't see the baby anymore. Adele knew that Sasha was a gentle loving dog. In an attempt to shut Sasha up I coaxed Adele into setting the car seat on the floor as I held onto Sasha. Very slowly I let Sasha approach the baby, she sniffed and pawed gently at her. Sasha finally calmed down but still wanted to be as close to the baby as possible.

Once we realized that Sasha meant no harm to the baby we continued our conversations. Sasha stayed as close as she could to the baby and eventually we quit looking down at them. It was time to go downstairs for snacks so Adele started to pick up the car seat, much to all our surprise we found Sasha had managed to snuggle into the car seat and under the blanket with the baby. Sasha was petting the baby by stroking her face with her paw. I wish I had a camera because Sasha didn't want to get out of the car seat so we carried her and the baby in the car seat downstairs together. When Adele was gathering her things to leave I had to forcibly remove Sasha and she was none too happy about it.

In June of 2002 another friend and co-worker, Angela, came over with her three-month-old baby girl. I had been teaching Angela to quilt prior to the birth of her daughter and this was the first time she was bringing the baby over to our home. The baby couldn't crawl yet so we were safe leaving her on a blanket on the carpet in the living room. My sewing room was now downstairs in the room Sasha and I had shared when she was unable to walk. We had removed the carpet from the bedroom floor to make it easier to roll around on my chair between sewing machines. We could see the baby in the living room from where we were sitting in the sewing room.

Sasha never left that baby's side. I swear we heard Sasha cooing to the baby. The baby was not asleep and was on her belly making little noises. Sasha appeared to be listening and responding as she was facing this angel cocking her head from side to side. Eventually this darling baby girl fell asleep with Sasha snuggled up right next to her having pulled the corners of the baby blanket up around them. I sometimes regretted not letting Sasha have puppies. I think she would have been an incredible mother. Again, Sasha was none too happy when Angela gathered her things and the baby to leave.

Even though Sasha had an affinity for babies, she loved all children. She seemed to sense they were special and became protective and nurturing around them. We always found this odd as we do not have children and it was rare when they were around our home. Sasha became a different being when around children – she wanted to be one of the children – not a dog.

Sasha, Extraordinary Dachshund

"What counts is not necessarily the size of the dog in the fight; it's the size of the fight in the dog."

Dwight D. Eisenhower

Paralyzed

In middle August 1997 Sasha started showing symptoms of weakness in her lower back again. She didn't want to jump up on the furniture to be in my lap and she was clumsy on our steps. I scheduled an appointment, and on August 25, 1997 we visited Broadway Veterinary Hospital. I knew Dr. Sessions was on vacation but I wanted Sasha examined immediately. I believe it was Dr. Baker who took a series of x-rays, confirmed our suspicions and prescribed the same medications and confinement that had been effective two years prior. Unfortunately, Sasha's condition worsened so I called the office in distress; they called Dr. Sessions at home. And being the goddess that she is, came down to the clinic on a Friday evening to examine Sasha.

During this examination Dr. Dawn mentioned there may be "alternative treatments" if Sasha failed to respond to confinement and medication. At this point she could do nothing more but stressed that we keep Sasha in her crate and immobile to let the medications work through her system. She instructed me to bring Sasha back in Monday morning.

By Saturday morning Sasha's back end was "down". She couldn't move her back legs or raise her hind end so she would not even attempt to walk. She couldn't wag her tail and she peed herself. I knew Dr. Dawn was leaving town early Saturday morning for the weekend so Mel and I took Sasha to the emergency veterinary clinic. The veterinarians examined her for deep pain, reflexes and muscle tone. Fortunately her muscle tone was good. However, they reported she did not respond to the deep pain test of squeezing between her toes with a pair of pliers. I was not in the exam room when this was done as humans were not allowed in the emergency exam room. Which may have been a good thing as I am not sure I could have remained calm or level headed if I witnessed someone squeezing Sasha's foot with pliers. The doctor's injected Sasha with pain and muscle relaxing medications, brought her back out to us and advised us to follow up with Dr. Sessions Monday morning.

First thing Monday morning we were at Broadway Veterinary Hospital. Even though Sasha howled at the sound of Dr. Dawn's voice, she couldn't wag her "happy factor" or remain standing on all four legs. Sasha's rapid decline perplexed Dr. Dawn; she felt it was necessary to get Dr. Eld of Mountain View Animal Hospital, a dachshund specialist, to examine her as a possible surgery candidate. She also mentioned Dr. Debra Mack as an alternative veterinarian if Dr. Eld would not treat Sasha. Dr. Dawn personally called

Mountain View Animal Hospital to request an evaluation of Sasha from Dr. Eld. Their staff called Dr. Eld with the request and he agreed to come in the next day just to see Sasha. Dr. Eld was the only dachshund specialist in our Treasure Valley. At this time he was mostly retired and only came in for very special problems with dachshunds. I was so grateful Dr. Eld agreed to meet with us to assess Sasha.

Even though Sasha was not feeling any pain, I was in agony and she could sense that. She gave me one of those looks as if trying to say, "the world is not coming to an end, be patient, and I'll be OK." I never understood how Sasha could be so matter-of-fact about the whole ordeal. Just as he always did, Mel stepped it up and took care of my responsibilities for the remainder of the day so I could just hold Sasha. Mel seemed to understand that when things weren't right for Sasha, they weren't right for me either. It was best to just let us comfort each other. Sasha never panicked or complained, she just accepted this is how it was and went with the flow.

We were now at that critical post injury 72-hour Golden Window of time.

Dr. Dawn explained the Golden Window to me as: The point of a paralysis in which an animal cannot feel superficial pain – a mild numbness, but when the toe is pinched hard, they can still feel deep pain. If an animal exhibits any kind of pain with a blown disc, we consider that is still within a golden window to do surgery. The surgical outcome is better than past the golden window when they feel no pain and complete numbness. The deep pain and complete numbness test is given by pinching, very hard, the web between an animal's toes with pliers. Most surgeons will not operate if the animal does not exhibit pain or pull back their legs in response to the fact you have pinched the toe to a bloody stump.

Sasha had no response to Dr. Dawn squeezing her back right paw with pliers! I did though, the blood drained from my face as I gasped in astonishment at Sasha peacefully sitting there happy as all get out because she was with Dr. Dawn. Watching Dr. Dawn continue to squeeze those pliers made me sick at my stomach. Sasha may not have felt the pressure of those pliers, but I did, I felt it in my heart. In that brief moment reality was cruel, I was confused, scared and heartbroken and I felt all the pain that Sasha should have been feeling.

CJ Adams

Our Appointment with Dr. Eld

I recall the appointment was set for 2:00pm. Naturally I was early and Dr. Eld was a bit late. In fairness to Dr. Eld, keep in mind he was mostly retired and was doing me a huge favor by just coming in. Time was critical, Sasha had been fully down over 72 hours at this time. Sitting in that waiting room with Sasha in her crate on the seat next to me, the gravity of the situation hit me. I started crying, softly at first then a bit harder. A beautiful little girl about five years old approached, looked into the crate at Sasha then up at me and said with certainty,

"Don't cry, they can fix her."

This angel was so sincere and was deeply affected by our situation. I thought about what she said as she turned her eyes away from me to look at Sasha in the crate and spoke softly, with the same certainty,

"You'll be OK pretty puppy."

I lost complete control of my emotions watching her assure Sasha that all would be well and just wishing it would be that simple. I started to really cry and this

77

seem to scare the little angel who went back to her mother and asked,

"They can fix her can't they Mommy?"

I totally lost it and started sobbing and then began to hyperventilate.

The angel's mother looked at me with understanding and concern. It seemed everyone in that waiting room wanted to comfort me. The staff realized my emotions were beyond my control and came to get Sasha and me to take us to an exam room. Another veterinarian came in to the exam room concerned that maybe I needed a treatment and even gave me a small brown paper bag to breathe into. I was able to barely put it together enough to communicate that I would be okay and how appreciative I was of their kindness.

Sasha and I remained in that exam room for about ten minutes until Dr. Eld arrived. I had never met Dr. Eld but was not at all surprised by this grandfatherly gentleman approaching us with sincere concern in his eyes. He was such a gentle, caring man who understood my pain and assured me he would do his best to help Sasha. After examining all the x-rays I had with me he decided to take another one to look for any changes. They were not good. There was no improvement. I could sense that Dr. Eld was looking for a solution because he was thinking and petting Sasha and you could tell he wanted to cure her. As upset as I was it was beautiful to see this kind doctor absent-mindedly stoke Sasha as he thought. Dr. Eld presented three options as he stroked Sasha's back: do nothing and see what happens, perform surgery and hope for the best or administer alternative medicine/treatment.

Dr. Eld explained that sometimes, without explanation, dachshunds have suddenly recovered the ability to walk. However, with the amount of damage to Sasha's back and this being her second incident, Dr. Eld did not hold out much hope for spontaneous recovery. In our Treasure Valley area Dr. Eld was the only veterinarian willing to perform the kind of surgery necessary to repair Sasha's back. However, he said something I will never forget,

"I'll do the surgery. But to be honest, I don't feel cocky about it. The worst-case scenario is the surgery won't take and she will be permanently paralyzed. This is not such an awful thing. We can order a wheeled cart for her to get around on. And this is also not the best scenario, as history shows that after a few years Sasha's organs will begin to fail and this may become painful for her."

This didn't sound good to me for I couldn't stand to hear that something may be painful for Sasha. I'd do anything to fix Sasha and willingly pay whatever it cost, but I didn't want to put her through so much trauma without a better chance at recovery. I felt hopeless and helpless.

Dr. Eld excused himself to make contact with Dr. Sessions. In just a few minutes he came back into the examining room and asked me to come into his office so the three of us could discuss the options for Sasha. Dr. Eld asked Dr. Sessions if she thought I might be interested in alternative treatments. Dr. Sessions explained she had informed me that acupuncture was an option and recommended Dr. Debra Mack. Dr. Eld further explained he was aware that Dr. Mack had successfully treated another dachshund with the same condition recently using acupuncture and that he felt Sasha was a good candidate for the alternative treatment. Dr. Eld phoned Dr. Debra Mack that Tuesday afternoon and she agreed to see Sasha early the next morning. We had passed the 96-hour mark by then which was 24 hours past the "Golden Window." But now there was hope and I had something tangible to look forward to.

I did not have the ability to think about 'alternative medicine' at that very moment because all I heard was "hope" and that was enough. I could have cared less what others may have thought at this time and I don't think I had an opinion myself about alternative treatments. I could only focus on Sasha and HOPE and POSSIBILITY and RECOVERY. It was impossible for me to think of anything else. Almost as if nothing else existed in my world and my only purpose on this planet was to fix Sasha.

I put Sasha in the front seat of the car with the doggie carrier door facing the driver's seat then got in on my side, opened the carrier door, put my right hand on her little head and prayed to God for strength and guidance. From that moment on I never gave 'alternative medicine' a second thought. I had to believe there was something out there to make my Sasha whole again. It really was as simple as that.

Dr. Debra Mack

Dr. Mack was to leave that Tuesday afternoon for a small vacation, but time was of the essence in Sasha's condition and she postponed her departure to see Sasha early Wednesday morning. Of course, I was willing to be anywhere at anytime, so with Sasha in her crate we left our home in East Boise at 7:00am for our 8:00am appointment in Eagle. Dr. Mack's home was a newer ranch style house situated on a few acres on which a full veterinary exam clinic was built. We stepped in to the small waiting room and barely sat down when this striking petite lady, who reminded me of Jodie Foster, introduced herself as she was taking Sasha's crate from me.

Dr. Mack had caring, intelligent eyes. I could see her thinking as she examined Sasha. She spoke softly to Sasha explaining what she was doing and constantly telling her how beautiful she was and what a good girl she was being. I could tell Sasha was enjoying this attention even though she could not wag her tail. Watching Dr. Mack tune in to Sasha was comforting to me. She touched Sasha everywhere, her hands were gentle and I believe Sasha thought she

81

was getting a thorough petting, as Dr. Mack became her new best friend. Sasha was not at all upset by this stroking and probing. She behaved as though this was just another part of her day and all was well.

During this initial examination Dr. Mack had me feel the heat along Sasha's spine. As I rubbed my hand from Sasha's neck to her tail I could feel a marked difference in the temperature above and below the area of injury. Below the injury point her back was very cold, which amazed me. Dr. Mack explained to me how acupuncture relieves inflammation and pain by re-establishing the flow of energy through the problem area. Once the inflammation is removed, the pressure on the spinal nerves leaving the spinal cord is relieved which reopens the pathways of the nervous system.

Due to the fact that we had more than surpassed the 72 hour "Golden Window" of time with Sasha, Dr. Mack started immediately with a very aggressive treatment approach which involved injecting homeopathic strychnine in several of the acupuncture points on Sasha's spine. She inserted acupuncture needles along Sasha's spine, in her hind legs and feet then hooked two of the needles to an electrical current. With the electrical current running, she administered the homeopathic injections into several specific acupuncture points and then left the needles in place for twenty minutes. I stood at the treatment table with my hands close to Sasha in case she decided to move. Even though I knew absolutely nothing about what Dr. Mack was doing I didn't question anything – she could have sold me ocean front property in Arizona – all I could see was Sasha being treated – that meant hope and at that very moment I didn't need to think beyond that. Sasha was her usual wonderful self and cooperated fully and seemed to have enjoyed this whole treatment – almost like a day at the spa. After this first treatment, Dr. Mack instructed me to keep Sasha confined as much as possible, discontinue all pain and muscle relaxing medications and to return for another treatment on Friday morning.

The second treatment began very much like the first. Sasha was very happy to see Dr. Mack and gladly accepted all the gentle stroking and loving words being said to her. Even though her tail was not wagging you could see happiness in Sasha's eyes. Dr. Mack inserted the needles, hooked up the current and injected the homeopathic strychnine to a very cooperative Sasha. I stood at the treatment table with hands almost touching Sasha. About seven to ten minutes into this treatment I saw Sasha's skin ripple along her spine like something was crawling around under her skin. I had to calm myself, stay still and focus on Sasha but I wanted to do a happy dance and sing because I was sure this was a good sign. Dr. Mack was at her desk making notes and discussing a possible change in Sasha's diet with me so she did not witness this and I was sure my singing would make her banish us from future treatments. Then, to my amazement, Sasha attempted to stand about fifteen minutes into the treatment. She didn't make it all the way up but she tried. My feet and hips were moving and I almost screamed out "hallelujah" but I managed to stay calm and tactfully request that Dr. Mack turn around to witness if Sasha attempted to stand again. Sasha did not attempt to stand again during the remaining five minutes of this treatment. However, after the treatment, with the needles removed, Sasha tried to stand on the table and even tried to take a step, but she did not yet have the strength or coordination to do so. Her front legs were fine and she could stand and support her weight for a very short period of time, but still could not move her hind legs or wag her tail. I was to continue her confinement with short periods of exercise if Sasha was willing and return for another appointment in seven days.

On this trip home Sasha and I did sing , "You are my sunshine, my only sunshine!" During this week we changed Sasha's food to Flint Rivers' no preservatives, all-organic dog food. Sasha loved the new food. We still laugh at how healthy the dog food was compared to what we humans ate.

On the third treatment Dr. Mack placed the acupuncture needles without the electrical current or strychnine and did a very gentle chiropractic adjustment. Again, Sasha stood during the treatment, this time for a bit longer and with very little swaying. We put her down on the floor to see if she would walk. She tried and it was a bit comical to see her attempt to walk while her hind end just swayed, throwing her off balance and confusing those little legs. She would just drag her hind-end around on the tiled floor. While this was cute, it was also heartbreaking.

The amazing thing to me was how calm Sasha was throughout all these sessions. She seemed to really enjoy the acupuncture treatments. Sasha was sort of walking after the three treatments in this ten day period. It wasn't pretty, as her back paws were a bit sideways and her back-end would still sway some. These were not perfect steps, but they were steps. Even though they were awkward and clumsy they were beautiful. Sasha was beautiful and seemed quite pleased with herself. When her hind-end and back legs didn't cooperate she'd sit down, reposition her appendages and try again. Sasha could drag herself around but I could tell this was not satisfactory to her. She worked very hard to walk. Never discouraged or frustrated by her failures she kept at it. Sasha didn't have a physical therapist coaching her or telling her exactly how to do it. I could see her thinking about what to do and how to get her hind legs to cooperate. She would turn her head around to watch her back legs as if she were instructing them what to do. Sasha was such a determined little creature and I swear she was willing her legs to move. It was amazing to witness this.

During one of the sessions, while we were standing at the treatment table, waiting for the 20 minute timer to ding so she could remove the acupuncture needles Dr. Mack told me about a dachshund named Amos. She explained that Amos fully recovered from the same condition as Sasha had. Amos was totally paralyzed in his rear legs for several weeks before they started the acupuncture treatments and it took two weeks of treatment every 48 hours before he was able to stand. It also took much longer before he was able to walk, so she was very encouraged by Sasha's progress up to this point.

After each successive treatment Sasha's back legs straightened out more and more and her coordination progressively returned. That meant she could be allowed more freedom, but still no running or jumping. I still pretty much carried her anywhere the terrain was not level. Our home had raised entrances of about three feet, which meant traversing stairs to enter and exit both doors. Knowing Sasha's recovery would take some time Mel built a carpeted ramp about twelve feet long to cover the five concrete stairs leading up our stoop so she could go up and down into our back door. Sasha loved having some freedom again. She still couldn't jump through the doggie door so we kept that closed. Sasha had no problem informing us when she needed the door opened for her to go out or come in. In fact, I think she enjoyed letting us know as she developed a different bark tone for "May I go out, please?" At first the ramp was a bit of a challenge and going down was easier than coming up but Sasha soon mastered that.

Each session brought more progress and after about three weeks Sasha was walking normally on level terrain. After five weeks she could run up and down the ramp and even jump on the furniture. Once Dr. Mack saw how well Sasha was progressing, she designed a schedule that slowly increased the interval between treatments. When the interval between treatments reached four weeks we continued to treat Sasha on a monthly schedule for a year. Sasha always loved visiting Dr. Mack, and I learned so much about holistic veterinary medicine. Dr. Mack was first a conventional veterinarian but became frustrated with its limitations and decided to look for other options for treating animals. Dr. Mack received certifications in holistic medicine, acupuncture and chiropractic care. She was truly a complete veterinarian.

During this entire time Dr. Mack had been pursuing further study in human acupuncture and naturopathic medicine. After obtaining her Naturopathic degree and acupuncture certification she decided to shift her practice to focus from animals to humans. Though this broke my heart, Sasha had healed and it was no longer necessary to continue her treatments. Dr. Mack had opened a whole new world to me and I knew I would always use holistic medicine in conjunction with traditional medicine for my animals. Dr. Mack recommended another holistic veterinarian if it was ever necessary for Sasha to have acupuncture again.

Sasha, Extraordinary Dachshund

CJ Adams

Our Home Life During the Paralysis and Acupuncture Treatments

Sasha required constant confinement and I could not bear to keep her in that small dog crate all the time. Mostly because it deprived me of her charming self and deprived her of my loving arms and comfort. Since she was paralyzed Sasha didn't know if or when she had to pee or poo. It just happened and Sasha could smell it and this distressed her. I discussed Sasha's dilemmas with my best friend and fellow animal lover, Mary McKinney, while we finished our workday in the bus yard. Mary had the brilliant idea of keeping Sasha confined in a playpen. Mel and I didn't have children and we didn't know anyone who had younger children that could loan us a playpen. I decided would buy one after going home to check on Sasha.

I went home to carry Sasha outside and then clean her up and while doing this told her all about Mary's idea. Sasha seemed to understand that she would be in a better cage before the evening was done. However, before I could leave the house to buy a new playpen, Mary showed up and surprised me with the playpen she used for her children over fifteen years ago. She had rushed home to check her storage shed and found her yellow playpen.

This act of kindness was the beginning of a deep friendship between Mary and me. It is amazing what people hold onto and store and how handy those items are at the strangest times in our lives. Mary had to set it up because I had no idea how that kind of contraption worked. The playpen was absolutely perfect! Sasha could see everything going on around her and we could see her lovely face through the side netting. I loved this arrangement because Sasha could be still and safe yet not cut off from us. The playpen had a vinyl-covered pad so accidents were easily cleaned up. We put plenty of blankets in it for Sasha to snuggle. Polly was home and would constantly change out Sasha's blankets so she never had to lie in pee or poo.

Even though Sasha could see everything, being confined in the playpen was still tough on her. She was a lap dog and wanted to be in someone's lap all the time. I went home every day between bus driving

90

routes so I could cover Polly's lap and her chair in pee pads, pick up Sasha to let her lie next to Polly. This not only made Sasha happy but Polly was very thrilled. At this time Polly was scared to pick up Sasha for fear of causing more damage. Polly's days had revolved around Sasha for several months now and she didn't like for Sasha to be away from her especially when Sasha needed comforting. And most importantly those two had developed daily routines. It was bad enough not to be able to go out on their walks so it was very important for them to have their apple sharing time.

Polly was afraid of hurting Sasha so she didn't want Sasha to sleep in bed with her during this time. On this first evening, Sasha "talked" to Polly at bedtime and begged to be taken to her bed for sleepy time. This broke Polly's heart to the degree she wanted to sleep on the couch just to be next to Sasha. Polly was sixty-seven years old and sleeping on a couch would not be good for her back. We moved the furniture around in Polly's room to accommodate the playpen for sleepy time, however, this didn't work. Around midnight Polly came up the stairs to our room with tears in her eyes and said,

"I can't stand this! Our little Sasha is just miserable and whining to be picked up and I'm afraid to pick her up. I'd get in the pen with her if I could fit."

Still half asleep I came up with a solution. I couldn't fit IN the playpen but I could sleep on the floor right next to it. I grabbed a few pillows and blankets from the hall closet. Mel got up and moved the playpen back into the living room and helped me set up a sleeping area. He lovingly moved Sasha close to the playpen netting and snuggled all the blankets around her then covered me in blankets as I wrapped myself around the playpen hoping Sasha could feel the warmth of my presence. While Mel and I were setting up for me to sleep on the floor, Polly was busy making up the couch. She insisted on sleeping on the couch the rest of that night so Sasha could know both of us were with her. The carpeted floor was tough on my bad back, and Sasha was whining because she had no one snuggling with her. I softly cried myself to what little sleep I did get that night.

I hated this arrangement as much as Sasha did. The only reason she couldn't snuggle with someone was due to her not being aware of when she needed to pee or poo. I needed to sleep; I drove a school bus and was responsible for the safety of all the kids who rode my bus. I would have just taken time off work but these were the first few weeks of school and no one was permitted time off.

That second evening while eating dinner on the floor next to the playpen I told Mel that I was not looking forward to another sleepless night. Mel said,

"We have a spare bed down here. Why don't we cover the mattress with plastic then add a bunch of puppy pee pads and cover it with sheets? That way you could sleep in a bed and have Sasha with you." (Is my Mel brilliant or what?)

Bed linens and pajamas were washable so now we could snuggle and sleep together and this would comfort both Sasha and me. We quickly became accustomed to the crinkle and crackle sounds that the plastic and pee pads made when I moved around in the bed. Each night I would lay Sasha on her side with her head on the pillow, facing me. I awoke most mornings with Sasha encircled in my arms with her back snuggled tightly to my chest. I must have rolled her over during the night as her head was under my chin and I could smell her wonderful scent. This made me miss her sleeping with Mel and me. I had forgotten how sweet she smelled and how close she could get to snuggle. Holding her was the most comforting thing for me. As weird as this may seem I could feel her calm essence and her need to comfort me every night and I only wanted to be with her.

If love could heal her then surely my love for her would ensure she'd be healed. I loved my husband for thinking of a way to do what was best for us. Of all people, he understood most my devotion to Sasha. He also recognized Sasha's devotion to me. Mel may not have been very fond of Sasha sleeping in our bed between us but he fully supported me in wanting to sleep with her during this time.

Sasha couldn't control her bowel movements but we seemed to have discovered the correct time was in the early mornings. Every morning I stripped the bed while Mel carried Sasha outside for a little poo time. He would kneel down so he could keep his hands around Sasha's belly to support her standing and they would stay like that, sometimes up to ten minutes until she pooped. Polly would launder everything then remake the bed for us so we could do it all again the next night. We were a happy family doing what was necessary to make this time bearable for all of us. Fortunately this routine didn't last long. The acupuncture treatments progressed so well that Sasha was back in bed with Polly and in control of her bowels within a few weeks.

Sasha, Extraordinary Dachshund

Polly Leaving Us

Mel and I married September 1987 and within a few years had sold our home to move in with his mother in Modesto, CA. Polly needed us as her longtime companion, Jim, had just passed away. Jim suffered a heart attack in the doorway of their bedroom and Polly just couldn't bring herself to sleep in that room anymore. That house on Poppypatch was big enough to accommodate us with the modifications we made. Then in 1992, Mel's company offered him management of a HVAC warehouse in San Jose. Polly's sister-in-law lived in a senior community so she thought she'd love to live there instead of moving to San Jose with us. We sold her house, purchased a mobile home in the same senior community and settled her in. We moved to San Jose, renting a small home. After about year, Mel's company was sold and within 60 days all the management was terminated.

This was August 1993 and when we took the opportunity to move from California. Polly joined us in early 1995 and lived at our Boise Ave home until dementia took over her mind. She decided to move back to Modesto in November 1998 into a senior apartment/assisted living community. Modesto was Polly's home and that is where she wanted to be.

However, during her three-year stay with us in Boise, Polly was Sasha's constant companion. They were best buds. Polly loved Sasha with all her heart and even though she was slipping into dementia it never affected her relationship with Sasha. I found this peculiar because every other relationship Polly had established was affected – most of them negatively. But she never lost her connection to Sasha. I don't understand why and I've never discussed it with anyone but it seemed like Sasha was Polly's one constant in everything. That was why it took Mel and me by surprise when Polly insisted on moving back to California. Polly had mentioned it several time but we truly didn't think she would ever leave Sasha. After Polly left us it took about two weeks before Sasha realized she wasn't just on vacation. Sasha looked everywhere for her and went around depressed and moaning because her Polly was gone. I often wondered if Polly missed Sasha as much as Sasha missed Polly.

That is when Sasha started misbehaving, nothing major, just chewing on the TV remote and peeing in my favorite shoes. Sasha even opened the bottom kitchen cabinets, drug out pots, pans and Tupperware and chewed on them. I had never experienced this kind of behavior in an animal so I consulted my dachshund book looking for solutions. This was not normal behavior for Sasha. This book stated dachshunds can be vindictive when left alone and they need constant companionship. I had provided that companionship when we first got Sasha, Polly had provided that for the next few years. But now Sasha was home alone most days. Her misbehavior now made sense and there was a solution. We decided to get Sasha a companion.

Getting Squirt

Naturally, I was thrilled at the thought of another animal. Initially I wanted a large dog. A German shepherd, like Bandit, or a Doberman pinscher, like Slick would have been perfect for me. However, Sasha's health and well-being had to be our chief concern in choosing a companion pet. A large dog could inadvertently injure Sasha's back. Mel and I were both working full time jobs that didn't leave enough time to properly train a puppy. We felt it best to look for a mature, house trained, smaller dog.

I notified the Humane Societies in Ada and Canyon

Counties letting them know I was interested in adopting a dachshund or similar small breed. Over the next few weeks I received several calls from folks looking to adopt out Labs, Rottweilers, Pit Bulls and other larger breeds but no one willing to give up a small dog. One Friday evening toward the end of January 1999, I received a call from an elderly gentleman. He softly explained his wife and he had to give up their pets due to moving into an assisted living facility close to their children in Oregon. The couple had contacted the Canyon County Humane Society who in turn gave them my number. I questioned them on size and breed and they told me Squirt was a male Chihuahua mix they estimated was about seven years old and that they also had a Dalmatian. I explained Sasha's situation and informed them I was very interested in Squirt but could not take the Dalmatian so we agreed they would bring Squirt to my house the following day.

While still on the phone the elderly gentleman was softy crying and explained that giving up these animals was heartbreaking for them and asked that I take Squirt no matter what. They were going to take the Dalmatian to the humane society before coming to my house in Boise and couldn't take the heartbreak of having to take Squirt there if I didn't want him. I could not resist his pleas and agreed to take Squirt and that if I decided I couldn't keep him then I would be responsible for taking him to the humane society. I was so excited to be getting a new pet!

At the agreed upon time a light blue Buick drove into our driveway. The driver's door opened and a very frail, elderly gentleman exited. I watched as he shuffled around the front of the car to open the door for his equally frail wife. He leaned in to hand his arm to her and waited patiently as she shakily came out of the car. You could tell this was something he'd done for her for many years and I thought to myself – that is Mel and me 40 years from now. Next he opened the back door on the passenger side and grabbed Squirt's leash. Bolting out of the car was a very scared and way too plump Chihuahua/miniature pinscher mix dog. With Squirt cowering between them, they shuffled the few yards necessary to enter our back entrance gate. I could see the heartbreak in their eyes as they escorted Squirt into our backyard to meet with Sasha.

Squirt was the color of beach sand with a black mask around his face and his ears stood up at full alert. When I first saw Squirt I knew I would keep him because he reminded me of Bandit, as they were the same color with that black mask on their faces. This had to be some kind of karma. Squirt had long, very skinny legs holding up a beer barrel of a body and he was nervous and antsy. I can still remember the elderly gentleman shuffling around our patio telling me all about Squirt. I listened with one ear as I fell in love with this agitated dog running around our backyard. His wife didn't say much because this whole affair was just too sad for her. I learned they adopted Squirt from the Humane Society five years earlier and at that time believed he was two to three years old. Squirt had been picked up as a stray and the Humane Society staff believed he may have been abused, from the cowering behavior he exhibited to them, and then possibly abandoned.

They had named him Squirt, obviously fed him too much and loved him well as he was their inside lap dog. Throughout his telling me Squirt's story he was softly crying. I had fallen in love with Squirt immediately and knew, then and there, that I would keep him. The elderly couple thanked Mel and me profusely as they would be able to leave town that afternoon knowing Squirt was in loving hands. The gentleman escorted his wife out the gate, opened her car door and again, waited patiently, as she lowered herself in. He shuffled to his side of the car, waved at me, sighed heavily and got into the car. He sat there for a moment, unable to start the car as he was crying. I saw his wife reach her left hand up to softly stroke his face. Again, I thought – Mel and me in 40 years. I watched as they backed out of our driveway giving them a reassuring wave that they left Squirt in capable hands.

Sasha took to Squirt quickly, as she did to everyone. Squirt was not an alpha dog so it was fine with her to have a bud. However, Squirt was very agitated and resisted all attempts for either Mel or me to touch him, much less pick him up. Squirt did take to Sasha pretty quickly and went around marking everything he could in the yard. Mel and I decided to let Squirt get accustomed to his new surroundings in his own time. Sasha came in and out of the house all afternoon but Squirt never did. After dinner we decided to go get Squirt and bring him inside for the evening. We had to catch him and that was no easy task. He could move a lot faster than Mel and me. However, with Sasha's helped we got Squirt cornered and I was able to pick him up. Squirt was very scared and trembling as I carried him up our back steps. I put him down expecting him to follow Sasha inside.

We were surprised to see Squirt was not familiar with a doggie door. So I pushed Squirt through the doggie door right after Sasha went in. This scared the wits out of him. I opened the door and Squirt shot out of the house so fast I don't think his paws hit the ground. Sasha took off after him thinking this was some new kind of game or something. They ran around the backyard a bit then Sasha decided to come in again, Squirt followed her all the way to the back door but he was not about to go in the doggie door. We picked Squirt up and brought him inside hoping he would just eventually follow Sasha out the door. He didn't and would only go out when we opened the door for him.

Mel decided we needed Sasha to help teach Squirt the freedoms of using a doggie door. Several times during the next day Mel would go outside; I would be inside, with treats on each side to entice Squirt through that door. Sasha was such a big help. She'd bolt through, stick her head back out and bark for Squirt to follow. She'd jump in and out, again and again, so that Squirt could see how it was done. Squirt just didn't get it. During this lesson we began to wonder if Squirt's elevator went all the way to the top. It took three days before he fully got the hang of it. He was slow on the uptake, but he caught on and when he did he shot like a bullet through the door. I guess the only time he went outside with the elderly couple was on a leash so this big back yard was freedom and doggie heaven.. Squirt wasn't interested in the squirrels and he made no attempt to pillage the strawberry patch. He loved lying in the fragrant creeping Thyme I had growing between the rose bushes as ground cover. He found a spot he could see everything coming and going in the backyard and claimed that as his own.

Sasha, Extraordinary Dachshund

Squirt Gets Out

On his fourth day with us, late in the afternoon Squirt managed to get passed me when I entered the backyard through the gate. He took off like a scalded dog. The elderly couple explained he had done this a time or two but he always came back home. I was scared to death because Squirt hadn't been with us long enough to know we were his new home. More importantly, we lived on Boise Ave – a major street, and it was 5:00pm going home traffic time. I dropped my purse inside the gate and took off after Squirt. Mel wasn't home yet so I was the only one chasing Squirt down the middle of Boise Ave, a major arterial road in SE Boise.

Most of the drivers on this three-lane street accommodated this chunky crazy woman running around and moved over or swerved to miss hitting Squirt and me. After about five exhausting minutes, which seemed like an eternity at that time, running up and down and back and forth the street, an imbecile idiot driving a large GMC, medium blue, 4x4 truck decided to make sport of Squirt and me.

Sasha, Extraordinary Dachshund

I will never forget this sadistic man's face and how much joy he took in trying to run us both down. He was actually chasing me, menacingly revving his engine. I was dumbfounded and afraid of what this loser would do to Squirt and me. This jerk just kept at it, and when I caught a glimpse of him he was laughing and taunting me. I couldn't hear what he was saying due to the noise of his engine revving but I am certain he was not complimenting my running style. I was frantic, running with everything I had in me and he was right there revving his engine. My biggest fear was that Squirt would come bolting out somewhere and that blockhead 4X4 bully would just run him over!

My fear then turned into rage, and instantly I was angrier than I've ever been. I turned around to face this bully, all 5'2" of me and pointed directly at him, yelling obscenities that would make a sailor blush and bolted straight for him. If he were going to run over me he'd have to look me in the face to do it and I was no longer afraid of him or his big truck! Like a mother bear protecting her cub I charged toward his truck in the center turn lane. This must have surprised the tough guy as I saw his eyes bug out. I'm sure there was fire coming from my ears and lightning bolts from my eyes as turned to chase down this imbecile.

My poor frantic Squirt, honking horns and screeching tires flying past him at 35MPH, traffic was crazy! I made it up to the driver's side door only because the idiot was stuck in the middle turn lane and couldn't merge into traffic. This schmuck had the good sense to roll up his window while I was coming at him and just as I started pounding on it, he took off like the cowardly bully he truly was, causing another vehicle to drive up on the sidewalk not far from Squirt.

If I had a gun, or any other kind of weapon, I'm sure I would have used it against this idiot. Amazingly, all this drama was playing itself out in full view of dozens of people who did nothing to help as they sped by with obvious annoyance at this disruption during their drive home.

While confronting the threat to my life I had lost sight of Squirt and the car that drove on the sidewalk just took off. I was mortified by then. Standing on the sidewalk, panting and trying to catch my breath, I heard horns honking a bit down the road and bolted off in that direction, located Squirt, running on the same sidewalk. I was able to corner him in against a wooden fence and attempted to grab him. He was too quick for me and he was scared out of his mind so he snapped at my hands and took off across the street and in the direction of our house. Weaving in and out of traffic, horns still honking and brakes still screeching, I was exhausted. But I gave chase down the middle of the road again. I chased Squirt all the way back just across the street and down a bit from our home.

Completely out of the blue this white Mercedes pulls over, a gorgeous woman with long black hair flies out leaving the engine running and the driver's side door open. She comes running to help me give chase. She is in a dress and high-heeled shoes. I must have been quite a sight for her standing there dumbfounded and exhausted! Suddenly we both saw Squirt shimmy under a six foot fence and she yelled,

"Jump over! I'll stay on this side to grab him if he comes back under the fence!"

I'm only 5'2" tall but my adrenaline was pumping

so without thought I jumped up on an electrical box and over the 6' fence. I landed hard and stumbled then got my footing and cornered Squirt against the fences. He was exhausted by now, his eyes were wide with terror and he was panting heavily but I managed to grab him by the collar and picked him up. He was snarling and squirming to get down but I had super-human, adrenaline fueled strength and was not letting him go. Squirt was trying to bite me and I thought both of us just might have heart attacks at any moment but he was safe now, all was well.

I then realized I was in someone's backyard, with Squirt wrangled under my arms, so began looking for a way out when I noticed the side yard fence was only three feet tall and as I looked in that direction the beautiful lady was waiting for me. I handed a very traumatized Squirt to her on the other side of the fence and crawled over. For some strange reason, Squirt immediately calmed down in her arms. He did not struggle or try to bite this stranger. She gave Squirt back to me, hurried over to turn off her motor and closed the car door. We crossed the street and she walked with Squirt and me to our house. As we settled Squirt down in our backyard she told me that as she first drove by she witnessed some of what the monkey's butt in the 4x4 was doing to me. She looked up in her rearview mirror in time to see me turn around and run toward the cretin so she did a U-turn in that crazy traffic to come back because she knew I needed help.

I never did get her name but what she did for us was so extraordinary. I had no way to personally thank her so I wrote her a thank you letter, sent it to the newspaper hoping she'd read it and know just how grateful I was. This lady was the only one, in the hundreds of people who passed by this chunky crazed broad chasing down her dog, to help. She risked her own safety and the theft of or damage to her white Mercedes to help. She was an amazing soul!

It took me several hours to calm down and I noticed bloody paw prints on the floor so I gathered a very exhausted Squirt into my arms and checked his paws for cuts. Fortunately the cuts were all minor so I cleaned them, put on some salve and made him stay inside for the rest of the day. I sprained my right ankle from the daring fence jump but didn't notice it until later that evening. Mel missed all the excitement and arrived home about an hour after Mercedes Angel left. As he prepared an ice pack for my ankle his only comment was,

"I feel sorry for that truck driver if you ever see him again!"

Squirt never attempted to escape again. For weeks I looked for that truck, everywhere I went. It didn't have a front license plate so I could not track the lunatic down. But if I had, trust me, I would've maimed that blockhead in the worst kind of way.

Squirt settled in nicely and finally bonded with me. It didn't take him long to realize life was good at the Adams' household. Even though Sasha was MY baby, she was her daddy's girl, so now I had a momma's boy and that suited me just fine. The sun was surely shining brighter in our household.

Sasha, Extraordinary Dachshund

CJ and her best friend, Kim Sullivan, with Squirt & Sasha, 2000

Squirt and Sasha

Squirt weighed 24 pounds on his first visit to Broadway Veterinary Hospital but he looked healthy. However, I don't believe his teeth had ever been cleaned so we scheduled an appointment. I took Squirt for his cleaning and left him at the clinic early in the morning. At the end of that day I was paying for Squirt's dental cleaning when Dr. Dawn came out to tell me all went well. One tooth was extracted but the rest were in good condition. She mentioned Squirt was defensive and snapped at the technicians as they retrieved him from the kennel for treatment. She asked me to follow her to retrieve him from the kennel so no one would get bit. This was the first time I picked him up after leaving him at the vet's so I wasn't sure how he would greet me. I was thrilled to find my boy wagging his tail and barking when he saw me. I had no problem getting him out of the kennel and he wanted to be held in my arms, not put down on the leash. I was happy to carry him all the way to the car.

When I came home with Squirt I found Sasha anxiously awaiting our return on the back stoop. She was so excited to see Squirt and danced around him all the way into the house and to the treat jar. After I gave them both treats Sasha had to administer a thorough sniff job and Squirt was quite accommodating and seemed to be just as happy to see Sasha as she was to see him.

Squirt and Sasha were best buds. It had been a long time since I had a male dog and was amused by some of his antics. Every time Sasha peed, Squirt would go and pee over the same spot. Sometimes he wouldn't wait for Sasha to be done so he just peed on her, it was too funny. Sasha would turn around with an exasperated look on her face and tilt her head then bark at Squirt as if to tell him, "be patient, already." At first I thought this was a male dominance thing but Squirt was not a dominant dog. I came to realize it was Squirt's way of protecting Sasha by covering her scent.

It took a few evenings but Sasha and Squirt agreed on which side they would lounge on sofa with Mel and me, Squirt always on the left and Sasha always on the right. They were adamant about that and it didn't make any difference which one of us they sat next to, they had to have their positions.

After Polly left, Sasha came back to our bed and slept under the covers between us. Squirt slept very close to me, at first on top of the blankets but then he started imitating Sasha and crawled under the covers and he always had to be touching me. Poor Mel, now we had two animals taking up space in our queen sized bed. It just speaks volumes for how much he loves me.

My most favorite thing about Squirt was he licked my feet – it was glorious! I didn't teach him to do that, he just started one afternoon while I was stretched out on the sofa and I didn't stop him. He could lick my feet for an hour or so, it seemed like some form of meditation for him and I LOVED IT!

Squirt became as animated as Sasha and doubled the sunshine in our home as he developed his own 'excited to see you come home' routine. Squirt's excitement was different though; he seemed more desperate and relieved at my coming home. I now had to pick up both dogs, Squirt in my left arm and Sasha in my right, both of them howling as I sang, "You are my sunshines, my only sunshines," and danced the three of us to the treat jar.

Squirt also started showing territorial guarding or protection duty, as I called it. He never slept while Mel was out of the house and I was home alone. Sasha slept when she wanted to, it didn't make any difference who was or was not there. When Mel wasn't home Squirt would always position himself between the closest door and me. He wouldn't lie on the comfortable couch next to me or in my lap; he stayed on the hard floor. It took me a while to understand that he was protecting me. Once his daddy came home then he could just be Squirt, a momma's boy, cuddly and at peace, not the protector. Poor little guy, Mel was gone a few days and nights on a business trip and Squirt didn't sleep the whole time. Even at night he wouldn't get in bed under the covers, he just stayed on the floor at the door.

We always joked that Squirt rode the short bus to school but in hindsight I think he had it all figured out and may have been the smartest of all in our household. Protect and love Mommy and the world was his oyster...so true, so true.

Squirt did not play well with others; he didn't like children and even snapped at two of our friend's kids. He was OK as long as children didn't get in his face. Unfortunately our friend's children were used to Sasha when they were over so they assumed Squirt was the same. Squirt nipped them both on the face; two separate incidents and it barely broke the skin. But I made sure all children knew to just let Squirt come up to them, not to hug him.

On our walks in Kathryn Albertson Park, with Mary and her two dogs, Squirt was aggressive to other dogs and always positioned himself between oncoming people, their pets and me. I could not break him of this behavior. I certainly did not teach it to him nor did I encourage Squirt to be so protective. If Mel walked with us Squirt was just another happy dog out on a walk with his pack. Squirt was only protective of Sasha and me. I always had to have his leash because others could be tripped or get tangled up in his lead if he felt it necessary to protect me. Mary and I used to laugh when Squirt got his 'Rottweiler walk' on because it took a lot of effort on his part to look as big as he thought he was. Mary had Sugar and Lucky, mixed breed larger dogs and both were female. Squirt was never aggressive to Sugar and Lucky but being the only male in our walking group he took his protection duty seriously.

Sasha, Extraordinary Dachshund

Strawberries, Grapes and Broccoli

Sasha would eat almost anything but especially loved strawberries and grapes. We love strawberries too. Mel and I cleaned a section of our backyard for a vegetable garden and he built a raised bed for a strawberry patch. As the strawberries began to ripen I would go out each day to pick them but could never find the ones that were fully ripe. I was blaming the squirrels for the disappearing ripe strawberries and talking some serious trash about them to Polly as we worked the garden together.

One afternoon Polly and I were weeding in the garden and caught sight of Sasha checking out the strawberry patch. Sasha was on top of the raised bed sniffing each strawberry. She was our thief, sure as the sky is blue. Mel was not a gardener and left all the yard responsibilities to Polly and me. However, he was our "fix-it man" so we told him all about our little thief and requested he do something about it. Mel, being smarter than Sasha, devised a cover over the patch to keep her out. This was no easy feat as Sasha had proved time and time again that she could get into anything.

115

This first cover consisted of flexible PVC pipe bent over like an arch then covered with double layers of bird netting. We put rocks on top of the 4x4 pressure treated wood we used to hold in the soil. First attempt to foil Sasha failed as she just knocked off the rocks, scampered under the netting and claimed her loot. Next attempt Mel stapled the netting to the wood with a staple gun. Sasha was not deterred. Second attempt was a failure as Sasha just pulled on the netting until it broke then scampered under again. I swear to you she thought everything Mel did to keep her out was just another challenge she was going to conquer. Mel finally had enough of this game, went to the home store and came home with enough 4' chain link fence supplies to surround the whole garden. Fortunately Sasha was not a digger and I could finally harvest enough strawberries to make jam.

The squirrels LOVED the new fence. They were free to plunder our crops without danger from the terrorist dachshund that shared their yard. And yes, they tormented Sasha from the other side of the fence. It took the squirrels all of ten minutes to figure out that terrorist dachshund could NOT get through the fence. I kept expecting them to build a little patio to entertain all the neighborhood squirrels just to torture Sasha.

The grapes Sasha loved hung from a neighbor's fence that had vines planted inside her backyard. Sasha only took Polly down the dirt road behind our neighbor's home to check on the ripening progress of those grapes when in season. At any other time of the year she avoided the dirt road. When the grapes were ripe Sasha would stand up on her hind legs and pick them one by one. She never gobbled them or tore them off the stems. Sometimes the neighbor delivered grapes to us but Sasha still wanted to pick them one by one off the vines. I could give her a bowl of grapes, it just wasn't the same, and she wanted to bite them off the stems. And, yes, she taught Squirt how to pick the grapes. He was her imitator and shadow. If Sasha did it, Squirt learned to do it.

My friend, Mary, still laughs at Sasha drinking her iced tea when she left her glass unattended while we planted pea seeds. Mary swore Sasha was asking for more as she caught her licking the last drops off her whiskers. Many times after a long day of weeding and planting we'd treat ourselves to Peanut Buster Parfaits with caramel instead of chocolate from the Dairy Queen located just down the street. We used the drive through because they always gave Sasha a little cup of ice cream when she was with us – which was most of the time. Sasha's nose was long and we swear she had the longest tongue ever because she could lick all the way to the bottom of the tall plastic containers to get the last bit of caramel from our treats. When we had Squirt, we had to let him lick first because he couldn't reach all the way to the bottom and then Sasha finished them off. That arrangement seemed to please everyone and Sasha even waited patiently for her turn.

Sasha loved all vegetables except broccoli and you couldn't fool her into eating it even with her favorite cheese mixed in. Sasha would put a cheese-covered floret in her mouth; suck off the cheese then spit the broccoli out. If I gave her vegetable stew that had broccoli she'd eat around it. Broccoli was the only thing I can remember that she wouldn't eat. In case you are wondering how I know what people food she would eat, we fed her only natural foods during her initial acupuncture treatments. We took her off processed dog food completely and I prepared everything she ate. Dr. Mack recommended an organic dog food from Flint River and after she was cured we ordered that monthly. Since the food was organic it did not have a shelf life so had to be ordered in small, fresh quantities.

Mel and I usually split a banana and cut it in slices over our breakfast cereal most mornings. Sasha, then Sasha and Squirt, had a bite of that banana each time we had one. Then they got to drink up the tiny bit of milk we left in our bowls and sat down on the floor for them. Sasha and Squirt were never competitive with food but they were comical at times. Each got their own end-of-meal plate or bowl. After finishing up what we left for them on their respective plates, they traded places to lick the container spotlessly clean. Neither one of them ever left a thing for the other one to finish up when they traded places but they always traded and licked the plate all over.

A Bed for All

Even though she was an amazing animal, Sasha had normal dachshund traits in that she had to sleep covered up so our house was full of blankets on every piece of furniture. In the summer we replaced the blankets with sheets to keep her from getting too hot.

In bed at night she crawled under the covers and slept between Mel and me. If she got too hot she would crawl out and sleep next to Mel facing him. Her little body lying parallel to Mel with just her head on his pillow was the most adorable thing I could see. Sasha loved her daddy and thank goodness she didn't snore. If we inadvertently lowered the bed covers to the point she didn't have them up to her neck, she'd raise her head then reach down with her teeth and pull them up. If they were out of reach she'd just get up, go get the blankets and drag them up to cover us all. Our bed and pillows were as much hers as ours especially after Polly moved back to California. I've slept with dogs and even cats all my life and I have never had one settle themselves in like Sasha did. I gave her a pillow just for her little head but she wanted none of that – she shared with her daddy and that was that!

Sasha, Extraordinary Dachshund

When Squirt got too hot under the covers he'd just get up and out and curl up on top of the blankets in between Mel and me. What was annoying about this was he stood straight up, did the shaking thing therefore removing our covers, then clumsily found his way on top of the covers. This disruption caused all of us to reposition the blankets and ourselves and settle back down for more sleep. I am not complaining and want you to know I would gladly suffer that kind of sleep interruption again.

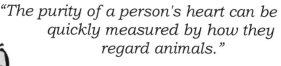

"The purity of a person's heart can be quickly measured by how they regard animals."

Anonymous

Squirt's Angel Returns

The most amazing event occurred in the summer of 2003. We were holding a garage sale in our front yard. I happen to hate garage sales so Mary was on hand to help me out. It was late afternoon on a beautiful summer day; we were sitting under a large shade tree in the front yard of our Boise Ave. home when this gorgeous long black-haired lady came in the front gate. Yes, it was she, Squirt's angel.

She said, "I was driving by, saw you were outside so I went to the store to get doggie treats and came back hoping to see Squirt."

Mary was just as stunned as I was. I introduced her as Squirt's angel but Mary knew, from my telling her the story, who this beautiful lady was.

I invited her into the house to see if Squirt would remember her. It had been three years since Squirt had seen this lady and that was only for a very brief time during his escaping trauma. Squirt is wary of everyone but, much to my surprise, he immediately approached his angel and greeted her with delight. This was the only time I witnessed Squirt behaving this way and all I can say is it was magical. She hugged him and kissed his little face and he never protested. Squirt enthusiastically returned her affections like he was a puppy. He was never that way with anyone, not even me. She visited with us for about 30 minutes and Squirt never left her lap. I learned she was leaving Boise for another job out of state. We properly introduced ourselves then but I still can't recall her name. I can tell you every other detail about her; just like I am sure Squirt could explain her scent. I cannot tell you if this wonderful lady smelled the same this day as she did 3 years prior but there was something I cannot define that made her special to Squirt.

What was it about her that made her unforgettable to Squirt? What was it about her that made Squirt completely drop his guard and love her so unabashedly? I thought about this for months but finally chalked it up to something I never would understand. I wish I could tell her about losing Squirt as she had a connection with him that was just theirs. She would understand my pain.

Squirt's Health

By October Squirt had been with us for nine months and had lost nine pounds and was a happy, healthy part of our family. Every now and then Squirt seemed to zone out for a few moments. Nothing dramatic or anything you could really describe to anyone. And it was Sasha's reaction that made me sense something was not quite right. I saw Sasha stand perfectly still, straight back and tail, staring up at Squirt and I remembered the incident with Susan and her epilepsy. I decided to call Dr. Dawn to set an appointment and two days prior to our appointment I saw Squirt have what I would classify as a seizure.

Suddenly Squirt lost his balance, stumbled around, got very shaky and appeared scared. It seemed like someone bonked him on the head and he staggered around a bit. It only lasted a minute but it frightened him. I scooped him up, held him real tight and sang an Elton John song to him. For that visit to the vet we took Sasha to be with him. Dr. Dawn ran all kind of tests on Squirt but we never did find out what caused the seizures. However we did discover that if you took Sasha along to the vet they could do anything to Squirt. That was the secret for Squirt, he imitated Sasha, and she loved the vet and now, so did he.

I know Squirt loved me because most humans would get a wild look in their eyes and two even called 911 positively sure I had self-amputated my arm when they heard me sing; but strangely enough it seemed to comfort him. I am hearing-impaired and know I cannot carry a tune in a bucket but music soothes the savage beast – even awful sounding music – and it worked for Squirt. He seemed fond of Elton John songs, which was good because I knew all the words to all his songs.

Sasha hated to see Squirt during these seizures and you could tell they really affected her. When I would scoop Squirt up and sing to him I had to sit down so Sasha should be looking into his face. After the seizure was over I would put a very exhausted Squirt down and Sasha would immediately snuggle next to him and lick his head. Even though they were the best of buds they never snuggled at any other time. Sasha had a gift of wanting to comfort everyone. She would stay by Squirt's side for a few hours after each seizure. There was no rhyme or reason for these seizures. And I am sure they occurred when we were away from home. The only way we knew a seizure was imminent was to watch Sasha's behavior. If she froze in front of Squirt then I picked him up to sing and snuggle until it was over. Some lasted 30 seconds and some from two to four minutes.

In February 2003 Squirt was limping a bit and was slow to traverse the stairs. He would leak a bit groan in pain when I picked him up. Dr. Mack was no longer treating animals so Dr. Dawn referred us to Dr. Jacquie Allgire of Healing Wise Holistic Veterinary Clinic. At his first appointment Squirt was his usual timid self and not very cooperative when Dr. Allgire started acupuncture for his back and his leaky bladder. However, after a few treatments, Squirt came to accept these treatments and to love Dr. Allgire. Squirt was back to his normal self within a few weeks but we continued to see Dr. Allgire for his leaky bladder and just general well-being for the remainder of his life. Squirt loved his time in Dr. Allgire's clinic and I really think he understood this treatment was good for him.

I took Sasha along when Squirt was being treated at Healing Wise Holistic Veterinary Care. The small waiting room had an aquarium situated in a corner between the chairs. Dr. Jacque only treated one patient at a time so we left Sasha in that waiting room while I handled Squirt during his treatment. After the first treatment, Dr. Jacque and I took Squirt into the waiting room and found Sasha on top of the aquarium biting into the water at the fish. If the top had been fully open I believe she would have just jumped in. Sasha was none too happy at being plucked away from the top of that aquarium and I was laughing while scolding her and telling Dr. Allgire of her obsession with fish. From then on I took Sasha in the treatment room with Squirt. It was always comical every time we entered the building Sasha went straight for the fish.

Dr. Allgire kept treats in her lab coat pockets and gave one to Squirt at the end of each session. After his second treatment I was putting Squirt's harness on and gathering up Sasha and their leashes to leave. Squirt was very distracted as he wanted another treat and was struggling against my efforts to hook his leash onto the harness. Dr. Allgire said, "

"Let him go so he can come say goodbye to me."

I let him go, he went straight back to her and sat down in front of her feet and she said,

"I got your number, little boy, and it's right here in my pocket," then she gave him another treat. From that session on after Dr. Allgire finished with acupuncture she gave Squirt a treat and then when I was finished putting his harness on he went back to say goodbye and got another treat. Sasha didn't care about the treats at all; all she wanted was the fish!

CJ Adams

"Be an advocate for your pet."

Dr. Patricia Saras, DVM

Holistic Veterinary Medicine

To be involved in the alternative treatments and therapies administered to both Sasha and Squirt was an amazing experience for me. Veterinarians have used acupuncture on horses for hundreds of years and now to witness it cure Sasha of paralysis and help Squirt through his issues convinced me that there was definitely something to alternative medicine. Neither Sasha nor Squirt had preconceived ideas about any type of treatments. They couldn't be persuaded from outside sources that acupuncture and chiropractic adjustments were voodoo medicine. Holistic treatments gave my precocious Sasha back to me, just like nothing had ever happened, and it was worth every cent because we gained almost ten more wonderful years with her. It gave my Squirt a better quality of life that helped him to live a bit easier in his final years.

At Dr. Dawn's request, I had kept her informed of all Sasha and Squirt's alternative treatments. Dr.

Dawn was intrigued with the healing process and was glad to have her patients benefit from unconventional treatment. She and I discussed at length as to why I was not aware that such holistic treatment was available for my pets back when Sasha was first injured. Dr. Dawn explained that our local veterinary board was convinced there was not true science behind acupuncture but that I could present Sasha's case to them, in writing, for review. I did write a letter for that purpose and gave it to Dr. Dawn to present to the veterinary board. I like to think that Sasha's case had a little to do with Dr. Dawn hiring a holistic veterinarian to practice at Broadway Veterinary Hospital.

Of course, after our first successful adventure I told anyone who would listen about Sasha, Amos, Dr. Mack and holistic veterinary medicine. Years later, while working in the advertising department of The Idaho Statesman I learned we were going to publish a pet edition in THR!VE, a weekly supplemental. I immediately went to the assigned editor of the project, informed them of Sasha's success and holistic veterinary medicine and encouraged them to investigate this and contact practicing holistic veterinarians. Fortunately, for all the uninformed pet owners in our areas, the first THR!VE Pet Edition had a story on alternative and holistic animal treatments. I was very satisfied that the general public now could read there were many options available to them for treating their beloved pets.

Holistic Veterinary Medicine, as defined by The American Veterinary Medical Association is "a comprehensive approach to health care employing alternative and conventional diagnostic and therapeutic modalities. In practice, it incorporates but is not limited to the principles of acupuncture and acutherapy, botanical medicine, chiropractic, homeopathy, massage therapy, nutraceuticals and physical therapy as well as conventional medicine, surgery and dentistry."

After much research on holistic veterinary medicine for this book and interviews with Dr. Patricia Saras, DVM, Dr. Rebecca Paulekas, DVM, MPT and Dr. Sessions I discovered there is so much more to this field than what I was exposed to with Sasha and Squirt. Holistic veterinarians are traditional veterinarians who take additional training to become certified in acupuncture, homeopathy and chiropractic disciplines in order to practice holistic veterinary medicine. Dr. Mack, Dr. Allgire and Dr. Saras all stated they decided to practice holistic veterinary medicine because they became frustrated with the limitations of traditional veterinary medicine.

With traditional veterinary medicine your pet is treated for symptoms usually presented at the time treatment is sought. Holistic veterinary medicine looks further into the animal as a "whole" to achieve a maximum well-being of your pet's health. This involves working with your pet's diet, environment, age, activity level and breed dispositions. A holistic veterinarian attempts to find the *root* cause of the presented pathology and design a treatment plan to address the symptom and the cause.

Not only is acupuncture an effective treatment for a current condition but it can be used as a preventative or therapeutic medicine like I did with both Sasha and Squirt. During the first acupuncture treatment Sasha received, Dr. Mack demonstrated the Chinese medical theory of *ch'i* to me. She had me rub my hand all over Sasha feeling for temperature differences. From Sasha's head down to the L1-L2 region she was warm. As soon as I rubbed my hand over the L1-L2 area her skin felt cold including her tail and back legs.

Ch'i is the life force that flows through a body along invisible channels known as meridians. There are fourteen of these meridians and they surface at some 360 places that have been identified as acupoints – the points where the needles are inserted. Acupuncture restored the balance of Sasha's *ch'i* allowing the energy to flow, uninterrupted throughout her body. The hair thin needles were inserted along the meridians at the acupoints, stimulating endorphins and allowing the energy to flow through and around the regions. The depth of needle insertions, the type of stimulation and the duration of treatment vary according to the type of disease being treated.

The holistic approach to medicine uses the symptom as a guide of where to look for the root cause of a problem. Acupuncture is just a part of holistic treatment. Sometimes it may be all that is necessary to achieve relief or a cure. Other types of holistic veterinary medicine include:

Homeopathy - the treatment of disease using minute doses of natural substances that claim to cause similar effects to the symptoms being presented;

Chinese herbs - used for balancing a patient's internal *yin* (cold) and *yang* (hot) meridians;

Chiropractic manipulation - used to adjust spinal joint abnormalities and neurological dysfunction caused by impinged nerves.

Dr. Saras explained that most people seeking her services are doing so because they have exhausted all avenues available in traditional veterinary medicine. Many times that is just too late. This is what is most frustrating for her. I explained to Dr. Saras how angry I was when I first realized there were options available for Sasha that I was unaware of. I considered myself very involved in my pet's healthcare and even I had no idea about alternative treatments and I asked her,

"Okay then, what do we need to know to change this situation?" Dr. Saras replied,

"You need to be an advocate for your animal. You need to be the one that takes on the responsibility of keeping them healthy, whether it is the food they eat, the medical care they receive or the exercise they get. They depend on you."

Dr. Saras further explained that it frustrates her most when an owner comes in seeking treatment for their pet at the last moment. To see their desperate hearts breaking, her knowing that death for that animal is imminent she just wants to ask them, "Why? Why did you let it get this bad? It was your job to protect this animal. Why didn't you seek me out before it was too late?" But she doesn't say it out loud, she understands this time is traumatic and she can only hope that next time they seek alternative treatment before it is too late.

My own frustration came while researching dachshund websites. I found one site devoted to wheeled carts for paralyzed dachshunds. I stayed on the site for hours reading the testimonies of owners being thrilled to still have their dachshund after surgery, even though they were paralyzed. I am fully aware that not all dachshunds can be cured like Sasha was. What angered me was that not one of the 100-plus testimonials I read mentioned seeking acupuncture treatments when their dachshund "went down." Not one person mentioned their vet discussing alternative options.

As I read through story after story from very devoted owners my heart started hurting for all those dachshunds. I even yelled at my computer screen, like they could hear me, "Are you people stupid or what??" But then I realized that stupidity had nothing to do with it. It was just plain lack of knowledge. I had been in that position also. These owners loved their dachshunds as much as I loved Sasha or they wouldn't have invested the time and money necessary to hold onto them a bit longer.

After realizing how many owners still remain unaware I had to talk to Dr. Dawn. We met for a few beers (she still likes Bud Light) to discuss this memoir and I asked what made her recommend alternative therapy to me, over thirteen years ago, and she replied,

"Number one, you had an open mind. Number two, back surgery is scary and expensive so why not try it?"

She continued by explaining that she regularly observes pet owners project their own experiences and beliefs onto their pet. If an owner had a bad experience with any type of procedure they won't even consider it for their animals. Dr. Dawn said she could tell I had an open mind because of our four-year history prior to Sasha's paralysis but then she surprised me by saying,

"Sasha was different, she was an old soul and I had

a special bond with her. I felt she just wouldn't do well with surgery. Dr. Eld confirmed that when he refused to perform the surgery."

I had to ask, "So do you think there is truth in the saying all dogs go to heaven?"

She replied, "I don't know for sure but I do know dogs have souls. Why else do people who have near-death experiences see dogs along with their relatives when they go toward the light? Check it out, they never mention any other kind of animal, only dogs."

I asked if she could tell the difference in regular dogs and extraordinary dogs – were all dogs extraordinary or was it just their owner's beliefs that made them seem so? She replied,

"It has nothing to do with you or your bond with Sasha, it was all Sasha."

(So much for her sensitivity to my ego.) She went on to say,

"Sasha could look deep into my eyes – most dogs never look into my eyes. Why did she do that and other dogs didn't? I can't explain it, something s are weird and I sometimes wonder if animals are on a different plane. In over 20 years of practicing veterinary medicine I have only treated five dogs like Sasha. Trust me when I tell you they are not all special like she was."

I recognized back then how bold Dr. Dawn had been when she recommended I seek out a complementary treatment plan. She is still bold and regularly recommends holistic treatments to this day, if the owner is open minded, as Sasha's success was just the first animal she co-treated. The referrals haven't always produced a success story and there are many factors that determine if she makes a recommendation. She stresses the number one factor being an owner with an open mind, next she considers the costs compared to traditional treatment as holistic treatments are generally less expensive and then she always looks back on her own experiences working with holistic veterinarians and previous successes or failures. Dr. Dawn definitely takes an alternative treatment referral seriously.

I expressed my disappointment to Dr. Saras that it seemed things had not changed much over the last decade in the way traditional veterinarians viewed holistic or alternative medicine. Dr. Saras was sad as she agreed and said,

"Unfortunately most people learn about holistic veterinary medicine through their own endeavors or by asking friends for advice. Some traditional veterinarians will refer a patient to me but it is usually only for therapy, after an unsuccessful treatment, not as a complementary treatment when the symptom first presented."

Acupuncture is the main form of holistic veterinary medicine I am familiar with but I want you all to know that holistic veterinary medicine is much more broad than that. Pets are successfully treated for cancer symptoms, skin rashes/diseases, digestive system irregularities, immune system deficiencies and aging related complications. I asked Dr. Saras what one piece of advice she would give you readers and her response was,

"Start with your animal's diet and get a really good dog food, supplement it with fatty acids and add natural enzymes. Minimize vaccinations and remember your animal is as unique as you are. Their health needs to be treated individually not just as a pet who presents the same symptoms as another animal."

Dr. Rebecca Paulekas, DVM, MPT agrees with Dr. Saras' advice about nutrition. Dr. Paulekas is one of only three veterinarians to have obtained a Masters in Physical Therapy and she is also board certified in Veterinary Manual Therapy and Medical Acupuncture. Dr. Paulekas explained that like most medical doctors, veterinarians have been poorly educated about nutrition. She has been encouraged in the last five years or so to see more research devoted to nutrition for better health of animals but stressed it is important for all animal owners to educate themselves and to be pro-active in keeping their pets healthy.

I asked Dr. Paulekas what advice she would give to every pet owner, she replied,

"I would say the best advice I could give anyone would be;

Get to know your veterinarian and practice preventative health maintenance with regular blood work and physical exams. Have your pet's teeth cleaned yearly, their dental health is important to their well-being and really impacts the quality of their lives. Having a physical exam gives your veterinarian the opportunity to spot warning signs and, as with humans, prevention can be much more cost effective than treatment.

Holistic therapy is wonderful for mature animals. Neutraceuticals can make a huge difference in the comfort and health as our pets age, but don't wait until they are old before you seek treatment."

Dr. Paulekas went on to explain that not all therapies work for all animals all the time but that she wished, "we could all embrace the therapies that do work." To her, and I agree, this requires the combination of traditional and holistic medicines that can be prescribed based on an individual animal.

I want to advise you all to seek out what is best for your animal. Only you know what that is and only you are responsible for that. I will always work with two veterinarians because both traditional and holistic medicines are effective and beneficial to the health of my pets.

"If having a soul means being able to feel love and loyalty and gratitude, then animals are better off than a lot of humans."

James Herriot

Soul - Intuitive - Sensitive

Some say pets don't have souls and are not capable of compassion or bonding with humans. I heartily disagree. How can you read about Squirt and his angel and not know there was something unexplainable going on? There are too many examples of dogs raising kittens, goslings and piglets to disprove that notion about compassion. It was because a human noticed their dog behaving strangely just before an epileptic seizure that taught us dogs can be trained to notify their human of an impending seizure. There are scientific studies about how dogs smell tumors deep inside a human body. I don't know if all dogs can be taught warning techniques to communicate with their humans but I know there are wonderful people working real hard to help that happen. You can check out any organization working with pets and I know each person would tell you of a dog with compassion, heart and soul. You may have had one yourself and if so, you were lucky!

There was no doubt in my mind that Sasha had a soul, in fact I would say she was an old soul just enjoying some time in a cute little body. I was not the only person who thought this. People responded to Sasha differently than they did other dogs. If they were lucky enough to spend any time with her they would comment about her being different, almost human.

A neighbor once asked, "Does she understand every word we say?"

I replied, "I don't think so but I'm sure she understands the feelings we are projecting in our conversations."

I do know Sasha regularly behaved compassionately. I suffered with migraine headaches for several years while Sasha was with us. She seemed to sense these severe headaches coming on. It took several episodes for me to recognize her behavior changed before and during a migraine. For example, instead of lying in my lap she wanted to be curled around my head as a headache started. As the migraine progressed she'd pet my head with her paws and lick my forehead and temples with long soft strokes. This was the only times she ever displayed this behavior. Most migraines lasted from six hours to three days. For the long episodes I stayed in bed in total silence and darkness. Sasha stayed with me the entire time and according to Mel left my side only to pee. Mel said she wouldn't even leave me to eat so he brought her food up to her and that instead of sleeping under the blankets, during these episodes, Sasha slept next to my head.

Another time Sasha displayed compassion and sensitivity to my well-being was during my back surgery recovery in October 2002. After coming home, four days post operation, I required 24 hour a day care for two weeks. My Dad was here for the surgery and hospital stay, my sister was here to nurse me for those two first weeks and my Mom came for the third week. Their lives and routines disrupted, Sasha and Squirt took all this in stride. During recovery I could only sit up for very brief periods of time that gradually increased after the first two weeks. I mostly had to lie down. Prior to surgery and after my recovery, if I was lying down on the sofa then Sasha was lying down on top of me. During recovery neither Sasha nor Squirt attempted to lie on top of me. Since Mel had raised the couch so I could get up from it easier, it was too tall for Sasha to jump on. Sasha seemed content to lie on the ottoman next to the sofa. She was always close by and I was in her sights. It seemed she understood the pain I was in.

Her soulful expression saying, "I've been through this. With my love, you will recover."

I always found it odd that our spines were injured at the same vertebra. Sasha and Squirt never pranced around my feet when I was allowed to walk using a walker. Even after I quit using the walker neither of them would walk too close to me. Only after I could walk in a normal fashion did Sasha and Squirt return to their usual ways. Their coming home greetings changed during my recovery. Sasha sensed I couldn't pick her up to dance and sing all the way to the treat jar. Coming home from therapy I'd find both of them sitting very calmly on the back stoop, never attempting to jump on me and even allowing me to enter the door without them between my legs.

I don't think Squirt was sensitive like Sasha, but he was intuitive, in that he followed Sasha's examples of compassionate behavior. While Sasha could 'go with the flow' in all situations, Squirt wasn't quite as adaptable. Anything out of the norm made Squirt nervous and unsure of himself. Squirt always looked to Sasha for what to do when things around him were unusual. Sasha was a good example and teacher for Squirt.

My initial recovery period was over six weeks long and full recovery took about six months. Sasha and Squirt's behavior gradually went back to normal as mine did. Their constant companionship comforted me throughout my recovery process. I was very fortunate to have many friends visit during my recovery and they all mentioned the difference in Sasha & Squirt's behaviors. Mary even mentioned making a little nurse's cap for Sasha because she was always there and never left my side.

Prior to the surgery Sasha and Squirt would sprint up the stairs to our bedroom for bedtime and wait at the top landing for Mel and me to join them. The first night home from the hospital it took me a good five to seven minutes to get up those steps walking sideways, holding on to the handrail with both hands and my very strong husband standing right behind me holding me straight up. Sasha and Squirt waited at the bottom then came up when I made it to the top landing. They then waited until Mel positioned me in our bed before jumping up to join us. Squirt had always slept between my legs. During recovery he slept between Mel and me. How do our animals understand this? I never had to scold either one of them or get them out of my way or worry about tripping over them.

Sasha, Extraordinary Dachshund

"Dogs' lives are too short. Their only fault, really."
Agnes Sligh Turnbull

Losing Squirt

Just prior to Thanksgiving 2004 Squirt became lethargic and wasn't his usual self. The seizures were more frequent and he just didn't seem right. During the holiday I noticed he didn't want to eat much and he slept a lot. The unexplained and more frequent seizures made him real tired. Sasha stayed close by him constantly and I felt something was really wrong. I had scheduled a vet appointment and it had been three days since Squirt had eaten when we visited Broadway Veterinarian Hospital. Dr. Dawn had taken that day off so Dr. Baker ordered an ultrasound that showed Squirt's kidneys we beginning to fail, his stomach and intestines were thick and there was sludge in his gallbladder.

Cushing's Disease was the initial diagnosis. Medicine was prescribed and we went home hoping this would make him feel better. I took some personal time off work to stay home and be with Squirt. He needed me to comfort him and I couldn't stand to be away from my boy when it seemed he was so sick. The next day Squirt became antsy, he began snapping at imaginary flies and would race around the house for no good reason then lie down, exhausted but unable to sleep. As the day progressed he wouldn't lie down, he'd just run around, mostly in circles, with a crazed look on his face. He would calm somewhat when I held him but it got to where if I wasn't holding him he was running in circles. This couldn't be good for him so I called the veterinarian that Friday afternoon. Dr. Baker advised me to take him off the Cushing's medicine thinking his behavior was an allergic reaction.

I knew it might take a day or two for the medication to work itself out of Squirt's system so I held him constantly. Neither Squirt nor I slept Friday night, all day Saturday and Sunday. On the third evening Mel was concerned about my lack of sleep but knew I would not let go of Squirt so he offered stay up and hold on to Squirt on the third night so I could sleep. We called Dr. Dawn for an emergency appointment that Monday morning of the fourth day. Dr. Dawn was on vacation so we would be seeing Dr. Steven Baker.

Mel drove us to Broadway Veterinary Hospital as I held onto Squirt with everything I was worth. Dr.

Baker gave Squirt a thorough examination and noted his strange behavior. I explained that Squirt hadn't slept in over four days. Prednisone was prescribed and a sedative injected. Squirt seemed to calm a bit so we went home looking forward to some sleep. As the day wore on the sedative wore off, quicker than we expected. Squirt could not be still; he started racing around again, but this time with his head down, leaning to the left.

Mel drove us back to the hospital. Dr. Baker administered more sedatives and allowed me to stay and hold onto Squirt while the sedative took effect. It didn't so he administered more, still no effects. I hated to let go of Squirt for any time at all because when I did he'd race around the exam room at full run, with his head down like he was plowing something up. This symptom caused Dr. Baker to believe Squirt had a tumor in his brain that was growing rapidly or bleeding out. The "wheel-barrowing to the left" Squirt was doing was a classic symptom.

Now, I adore Dr. Baker, he had taken care of both Squirt and Sasha when Dr. Dawn was unavailable and he will be the veterinarian for me when Dr. Dawn retires. But at this point I needed Dr. Dawn to be involved. Something this serious renders me unable to think and she knows how to communicate with me about my pets better than anyone. It was the end of the day and the staff offered to call her in immediately. I declined stating we could wait until tomorrow morning to see her. They instructed me to come in early and called Dr. Dawn requesting she come in a bit early. They wanted to keep Squirt overnight but I couldn't bear to part with him. Who would stay up to hold him all night? Who would sing Elton John songs to calm him? No one could do what I could do for him. Mel drove us home on that cold winter evening.

Mel prepared our dinner. He held Squirt while I ate and took a nice long shower. No sleep for Squirt or me that night. Mel stayed up as long as he could and I had to beg him to go to sleep. It wasn't necessary for us both to be sleep deprived. I got comfortable with Squirt on the downstairs couch. Strangely Sasha didn't follow her daddy up the stairs, she never left our sides.

We hadn't taken Sasha to the hospital with Squirt through this whole situation and she hated it. As soon as we walked in the door with Squirt she'd scramble to get close to him. She tried to comfort Squirt by licking his head when I could hold him still long enough. Sasha had to be touching Squirt. This was a bit of a juggling act. My arms ached as Squirt struggled the whole time. During the brief moments that evening that I would let him out of my arms he raced around in circles as if he was possessed, you could not tell he was sleep deprived in any way.

By the time we saw Dr. Dawn on December 4th, it had been over five days of no sleep or food for Squirt. Mel managed to get Squirt into a small dog carrier for me, as he had to be at work. Again, leaving Sasha at home, I drove him to the hospital. I must have looked frightful but the staff seemed to exist only to comfort Squirt and me. Dr. Dawn came in early to review Dr. Baker's findings. And even though it is not procedure, they allowed me to be the one to handle Squirt throughout this joint examination.

After further tests and examination their combined diagnosis was a tumor bleeding out in Squirt's brain.

Without a CT scan to see exactly where the tumor was and access to immediate surgery Squirt could not be helped. The closest veterinarian hospital capable of operating on Squirt was in Seattle. Even though I was sleep deprived and mentally exhausted I knew I couldn't let Squirt suffer any more. If the tumor was bleeding out he only had a few hours remaining. There was no hope; Squirt was suffering so euthanasia was our only option.

In the euthanasia room Squirt could not be still, he raced around and around and wouldn't even respond to his name. He appeared to not even recognize me, and that was heartbreaking beyond words I can express. Dr. Dawn administered the drug while I was holding onto Squirt struggling to keep his eyes looking into my face. Squirt took his last breath in my loving arms. I don't think he was aware of impending death or me. To see his small body relax was a blessing for me. I know we all have pets and that they comfort us with their presence but I had to let Squirt go to bring him comfort. Owning a pet is usually a very selfish thing, they satisfy various wants and needs in our human psyche. But trust me, euthanizing Squirt was one of the most unselfish things I've ever done.

Dr. Dawn's assistant wrapped Squirt's warm limp body in a blanket and lovingly placed him in a small cardboard coffin for me as I chose to bury him in at home. Dr. Dawn and her staff comforted me by acknowledging we had done everything possible and reminded me how wonderful Squirt's life had been while he was my "special" boy. It was drizzling rain as I drove home with my precious boy and my heart was so heavy my chest hurt. It felt as if this gloomy December weather was grieving with me.

147

I brought my very special boy home to find Sasha waiting on the back porch for us. Sasha HATED the cold so to see her beautiful face waiting outside, with a look of anticipation at Squirt's return, was unusual. I was crying as I retrieved the coffin, seat-belted in the front seat, from the car. Sasha just sat at the top of the stoop, strangely still, with confusion on her face. The only time we came home to Sasha's tail NOT wagging was when she was paralyzed. I really needed a cigarette so I placed Squirt's coffin on the stoop next to Sasha, she immediately started growling and looked for a way to get it open. She did not like this one bit and whined and growled at me while I smoked.

I was so taken aback by Sasha's reaction I had to call Dr. Dawn for advice on how to handle Squirt's death with Sasha. She advised me to let Sasha smell and investigate Squirt's coffin because she would smell that he was dead and she would then understand he was not coming home and that this should calm her down.

My mother had given me a dogwood tree for my 43rd birthday back in February. I had dug this tree out of the ground, back in October, in preparation of taking it to our new home. It just seemed prudent to bury Squirt in that spot, however the hole needed to be deeper. I went to gather my gardening gloves and the shovel from the shed. Most of the gardening supplies had been packed away but I expected to easily locate my gloves. I dug through several boxes trying to pull myself together as this was the first time I was to bury my own pet all alone.

I had to go inside the house to call Mel to find out where he put the boxes with my small gardening supplies. This upset me terribly because I wanted to bury Squirt by myself. I had not lost a pet as long as I had known Mel so he was unaware that I needed to have a little funeral and bury them properly. I wanted to do this alone so as not subject Mel to my rituals as he was not a religious individual and hated funerals. And to be honest, I wanted to be alone with my grief. I was shaken to my core. Squirt was MY boy and I needed to do this myself. Mel answered the phone at Boise Golf & Tennis and as I tried to hide my sorrow I bluntly asked him where my garden gloves were.

Mel hesitated a moment then asked, "Why do you need garden gloves in December?"

I answered, "I just had Squirt euthanized and I want to bury him."

Mel inhaled, slowly exhaled then said, "Wait for me, I'm coming home."

"No," I said, a bit too curt, I want to do this by myself."

Mel softly replied, "That's not fair, he was MY boy too. I'm coming home so you just wait. I'll be home in less than 15 minutes."

I think Mel knew this might have been a possibility when he put Squirt in the crate that morning. I didn't have a choice but to wait for him and he had a valid point. Then I realized he was right, I was being selfish. I went back out to the stoop to find Sasha lying down next to Squirt's coffin on the cold concrete and started crying. It started to snow and was very cold and it would take Mel 15 minutes to drive home so I lit another cigarette and sat down next to Sasha to wait. It was just too cold outside to finish that cigarette and Sasha was shivering so I picked up Squirt's coffin to take it inside for the wait. Sasha was beside herself trying to get to the coffin in my hands jumping on my legs and whining. I went through the laundry room, dining room and kitchen into the living room. I placed Squirt on the large brown ottoman then plopped down on the sofa because I was exhausted to my very core.

Sasha immediately jumped up on the ottoman to sniff around the coffin and pushed at the lid with her nose. She seemed to want the lid off and would look back at me like I should understand what she wanted. I slipped the cardboard lid off to reveal my precious boy wrapped in a blanket, so peaceful and adorable that I began crying again. Sasha could see Squirt's head, as she looked in. She growled in a tone I had never heard from her before. More like a moaning in what I would call a mournful tone. She sniffed and licked at Squirt's face then positioned herself so that her chest, front paws and face were now on top of Squirt's chest. Sasha then took her front paw and started stroking Squirt's head around his ears. Oh my God, I lost it emotionally! Seeing Sasha behave this way was one of the most amazing things I'd ever seen. Sasha whined softly while stroking his head. I sobbed with my full being while watching the whole ordeal.

About three minutes after she started stroking Squirt's head, Sasha heard Mel's truck pull up and jumped down off the ottoman and bolted to the back door. I was bawling so hard I couldn't hear anything but my own grief. Barking, Sasha led the way as Mel rushed in because he heard me crying. Sasha ran passed the treat jar like she was rushing Mel into the living room. He saw Squirt in the open coffin and understood my sorrow. Mel looked down at me with his own grief so apparent in his handsome face. Then he sat down heavily next to me on the sofa and wrapped his strong comforting arms around me as I cried while telling him everything that happened at the vet's office.

After gaining my composure I told Mel what Sasha did and he became emotional. Sasha got back up on the ottoman and stood next to Squirt as Mel lovingly placed the lid back on.

Mel went to the shed to grab the shovel, not bothering with gloves, and started digging the hole deeper while it was snowing. It took Mel about fifteen minutes to dig in the frozen ground. Sasha and I stayed outside next to Mel the whole time. Once the hole was deep enough we placed Squirt in, together, and shoveled the dirt on top until the hole was filled back up. Mel gently tamped the loose soil to compact it and I stood and cried. Sasha walked around and around the grave for about ten minutes before she would come inside to the warmth.

This was Sasha's only exposure to death yet she seemed to understand that Squirt was irretrievably gone because she never went around the house looking for him like she did when Polly moved away.

I was absolutely exhausted and Mel had to go back to work. Sasha and I curled up on the couch to sleep. I cried myself to sleep with Sasha's face next to mine. She'd lick a tear away and sigh as if she understood and wanted to comfort me. We woke up five to six hours later at the sound of Mel coming home. To my surprise, Sasha was not curled up in my arms; she was on the ottoman, where Squirt's coffin had been. She had dragged a blanket from the sofa while I was asleep and was curled up in it on that spot. We were a very sad household. The gloomy winter weather lived in our hearts for a few days. However, we had to get back to packing as our home was on the market to be sold. This kept our minds and bodies busy. Sasha was an only child again at eleven years old.

My time was all too brief with this special needs lover boy, at only 4-1/2 years, but to this day my heart feels with joy just thinking about my boy Squirt. We commonly called him SquirterBirterDirter. It is weird but it fit him well. You can't say SquirterBirterDirter without smiling and I can't think of him without smiling. Squirt loved to lie in the sun on the scented creeping thyme planted between the roses. It was his spot and I think he loved the smell. Squirt loved to go for walks but didn't want to socialize with other animals, unlike my social butterfly, Sasha. Sasha ran towards every person and every other dog because she fully believed they wanted to love her. Squirt didn't want to be loved by others, as long as he had his Mommy that was enough for him.

Doggie Day Care

Our niece, Jessica, was getting married in August 2005 so we scheduled a two-week vacation to Fresno, California to fulfill a promise Mel made eighteen years prior. Jessica was a precocious five-year-old when I married Mel at her home in Riverbank, California. The evening before our September 1987 wedding, Mom and I were heavy into preparations inside the house. Jessica followed Mel around while he photographed us setting up the tables and making things beautiful. According to Mel, while he was taking photos of our wedding preparations little Jessica asked him if he would take photos of her when she got married.

This was the first time we could not take Sasha on a trip because we planned to visit Polly, who was in a hospice facility in Modesto. Karen, Mel's sister, and her family lived in Hickman and we wanted to see them also. We were planning to stay in motels the entire time and could not make reservations due to the uncertainty of when we'd be where. Since we lived in a senior community we could not hire someone younger than 55 to stay at our home. We didn't know anyone over 55 who was willing to live in our home during this

153

two week time period and I wanted someone with Sasha 24 hours a day. I looked into several doggy day care facilities months before it was time because I wanted Sasha to stay at one a few times before we left for two weeks.

I found the most wonderful facility online and was impressed by their website. I made an appointment at Doggie Daycare and Salon to visit the facility with Sasha. We arrived at a home situated on a large lot and met Kathy Brown. Kathy just had a baby and told me she also had a six-year-old son. She stayed at home with all the animals 24 hours a day. Their home had been modified for just such a purpose and it was immaculate, exceptionally organized and well designed. The drop off/pick up room was painted purple with Roman style columns and murals on the walls. There were couches; big fluffy pillows and lots of chew toys. Kathy gave Sasha and me a tour of the property that included a huge fenced backyard that was landscaped with dogs in mind. There was even a wading pool for cooling off on hot days. There must have been about eight dogs of different sizes and breeds at the facility on my first visit. Kathy had complete control of all of them. In answer to my concern about larger dogs being around my formerly paralyzed elderly dachshund, Kathy explained it was their practice to keep the smaller breeds away from the larger ones so Sasha would never come in contact with the larger dogs. Doggie Daycare had strict schedules about what breeds could be in the same area and I really appreciated this. Sasha was twelve and we had never left her with someone who was not staying in our home. This was very scary for me because I had never been away from Sasha this long, but I knew it was necessary. Sasha seemed quite comfortable is this facility.

I booked a weekend stay to begin with. Mel and I dropped her off early on a Saturday morning. Again, I found the place to be exceptionally clean and Kathy personally accepted Sasha for her weekend. There were a couple of other small dogs in the room and Kathy set Sasha down in the middle of the room. Sasha did her Queenly pose, allowing the other dogs to smell her. She in turn greeted them and it was time for some fun. Watching Sasha with the other dogs made me feel like I was dropping off a giddy 12-year-old girl for a slumber party.

I picked her up on Monday morning. Kathy told me Sasha was quite a hit with the family. It turns out their six-year-old son fell in love with Sasha so instead of bedding down with the other small dogs, she slept with him for the two nights. This is the first time they had allowed that to happen. Not only did she stay with the family instead of the other dogs she showed them just how smart she was.

Kathy asked if I'd ever witnessed Sasha problem solving. I responded, of course, but never mentioned it to others because they would think I was certifiably crazy. Kathy told me about this incident: it was dinnertime; they were all at the table with the baby in a seat that attaches to the tabletop. They already figured out that Sasha LOVES babies and wanted to be near this one. While having their dinner they observed Sasha looking around the dining room working out a route to get to the tabletop. Sasha figured it out and it must have been quite a feat because they were too stunned to stop her. Sasha got to the baby and sat with her in the seat. I was not at all amazed, I'd seen her do something very similar to this before.

Senior Living

Mel and I purchased a manufactured home in a mature living community. We moved in with our only child, Sasha, in February 2005. Our backyard is very small but has several mature trees lining a long natural irrigation canal. The water runs through the large, wide canal eight months of the year. For us, it is like living on a river and the sound of the rushing water is pleasing and calming. The huge trees on the slope leading down to the canal offer lots of shade and plenty of squirrel and bird habitats. Our bedroom is in the back of our home so most summer nights we can turn off the AC, open the windows and sliding glass door to be cooled and serenaded at the same time. It is just gorgeous but Sasha was interested in only one thing...the abundance of squirrels that called those trees home. Funny thing is she seemed to lose interest in them after realizing she was not free to chase them. Our community does not allow fences and pets must be leashed when outside.

Not only was Sasha an only child but her freedom was hampered by our move. Living at the Boise Ave house Sasha could come and go as she pleased with a very large backyard as her domain. Now her outdoor excursions required her harness and leash. Sasha loved her walks and we took her out every time she indicated she wanted to go outside. Our neighbors all adored Sasha's prancing in front of Mel and me on our walks.

Not even the most curmudgeonly senior citizens are immune to the cuteness of a dachshund. And Sasha was a charmer. She willingly accepted each compliment and affectionate stroke from her neighbors. Many of our neighbors have small dogs and they all enjoyed a quick sniff and romp as their humans conversed. As the first year progressed in our new community the walks became shorter and the pace a bit slower. Instead of taking off to chase the Canada Geese that peppered our area twice a year, Sasha became content to just bark a warning at them.

At this time Mary had a split-shift job so she stayed at our house for the three to four hours between times she was needed at her job. Mary had been Sasha's second Mom all her life so this suited Sasha just fine. When Mary couldn't be there, Mel and I took turns going home at lunch or break times, since both our jobs were about one mile from our home. We did not leave Sasha alone for more than two to three hours at a time. It was working out well and Sasha was happy.

I had placed a recliner next to the front windows to use as my spot to read books. Sasha spent many hours snuggled in my lap as I read. If I happened to be busy in the sewing room then she snuggled with Mel on the sofa while he watched movies. After each reading session I would place the snuggle blankets all over the chair so Sasha could see what was happening in the neighborhood while she comfortably lounged.

The neighbors assured me Sasha barked her greetings each time they passed by when we were at work.

Sasha could see us pulling into the driveway from her perch. I always loved approaching our home seeing Sasha's happy factor wagging at supersonic speed, then BAM – she'd shoot off the recliner and bolt toward the door to greet me. Even if I had a bad day or was in a bad mood it faded as I opened the door. My angel would be prancing around in circles greeting me with unbridled love and happiness. I'd pick her up and sing and dance all the way to the treat jar. I wish I could bottle that feeling and sell it as a cure for all things bad in our human lives. I'd be filthy rich!

As time progressed Sasha quit jumping off the recliner and bolting to the door. She'd remain comfortably perched in her chair with her happy factor moving at a constant speed. I had to walk to her but her greeting was still pure happiness. I'd pick her up and dance around still singing "You are my sunshine, my only sunshine." She'd bark her own version and we'd make beautiful music together all the way to the treat jar – it was our tradition.

It broke my heart to see small signs of Sasha aging. Squirrels were now safe and even cats could walk by without a barrage of fierce barking. Our little girl seemed to fit right in to our senior community. When we first moved here there was an elderly neighbor who took his small dog for a walk every day while he rode around in a golf cart and I told Mel eventually I'd have to get one of those carts – not for golf – but to exercise my pets as I got older. As time progressed I noticed that every now and then his mature dog would be riding shotgun in the golf cart and that made me smile. It wasn't much longer before their entire walk involved riding around our community in the cart. I loved that this gentleman still gave his beloved companion the thrill of being outside and visiting with others without having to be in pain.

I began to carry Sasha or put her in my bike's basket with pillows and blankets for outings and she loved these. I liked to imagined she felt like Ms. Daisy when in my bike basket and cruising around the neighborhood.

CJ Adams

"He is your friend, your partner, your defender, your dog. You are his life, his love, his leader. He will be yours, faithful and true, to the last beat of his heart. You owe it to him to be worthy of such devotion."

Unknown

Beginning of the End

It was July 2006 we began to see some of what we thought were signs of our 13 year old beloved Sasha aging. We schedule an appointment to visit Dr. Dawn to discuss aging issues and how to make Sasha comfortable and happy. Maybe it was time to start acupuncture again. I wanted her to be as pain-free as possible and to enjoy this phase of her beautiful life with us. Just prior to the appointment Sasha began vomiting, refusing water and had explosive orange diarrhea. She even started sneezing, which led us to believe she had a cold.

Mel drove us, with Sasha bundled up in my lap, to this appointment. Sasha may not have felt well, but she still got excited arriving at Broadway Veterinary

161

Hospital. As soon as Mel turned off the car engine Sasha was ready to get out to visit with her fan club. We walked her around outside to allow her to pee and poo. Then Sasha entered the building all perky with her tail wagging. We sat to wait our time and as was customary with Sasha, she deposited a fresh poop sample in front of the reception desk.

My favorite technician, Elizabeth, laughed as she said,

"Guess we'll take a fecal culture since Sasha is so accommodating."

I agreed to the tests. On cue, Sasha started howling upon hearing Dr. Dawn's voice. Dr. Down walked out of the exam room escorting another patient out to reception area. She was laughing while Sasha was howling as this never ceased to amuse her. The rest of us were just annoyed by this loud horrible sound emanating from my small princess. After finishing with the other patient, Dr. Dawn crouched down, rubbed Sasha around the ears and said to her,

"That is the best happy factor I've seen today. Sure makes me feel good to know you still love me! Oh and how accommodating you are to deposit a little 'present' for us to examine. What a good girl you are!"

Unfortunately for Elizabeth, this particular poop sample was runny, orange and smelled especially atrocious. Dr. Dawn instructed Elizabeth to process a full panel on the 'present'.

In the exam room, as Dr. Dawn looked into Sasha ears and eyes, she informed us there were several pet daycare facilities in our downtown area dealing with an epidemic of canine flu. I mentioned that Sasha had been to daycare a few weeks prior. But since Doggie Daycare is located far from downtown and Kathy had not mentioned having any boarders with communicable diseases, I wasn't concerned. Dr. Dawn, however, took the time to call Kathy to inquire if other animals were exhibiting symptoms. Kathy explained only one other animal had mild sneezing and coughing and it was a large breed dog. Sasha would not have been exposed to a larger animal. Dr. Dawn ruled out the canine flu and suspected Sasha was just suffering from a cold.

Dr. Dawn also noted the beginnings of cataracts in Sasha's eyes. Appropriate medications were prescribed and, as always, Elizabeth explained in detail how and when I was to administer them. We took our little patient home to recover and Sasha rebounded in reasonable amount of time.

However, this was just the beginning of noticeable differences in Sasha's demeanor and health. We had to pick her up so she could snuggle on the sofa or sleep in bed with us. Sasha had the energy to go out for a walk but got to the point where we had to carry her back home. Then her walks were just across the street to potty. By March 2007 her bladder was leaky and sometimes she couldn't make it outside before having to relieve herself. I found out Dr. Allgire had moved and could not locate another holist veterinarian so acupuncture was out. I phoned Dr. Dawn and she prescribed a bladder medicine, which helped tremendously.

In early June I noticed further degradation in her eyesight. Sasha was slow to alertness and seemed confused at noises she couldn't readily identify. I noticed some blood in her stool so we scheduled an appointment. Dr. Dawn took blood, examined her eyes and confirmed Sasha was losing her eyesight. The blood test results were back and we went for a follow-up appointment on June 13th. The results indicated Sasha had giardia and was showing signs of diabetes. For the first time ever Sasha refused her favorite treats from Dr. Dawn.

Dr. Dawn changed Sasha's medications and she seemed better for a few days. But, then she started drinking lots of water, seemed depressed and her eyesight seemed worse. At our June 23rd visit Dr. Dawn ordered an ultra sound. She also noticed Sasha was walking a bit gingerly and stiff legged.

The doctor qualified to perform ultrasound and interpret the results came to Broadway Veterinary Hospital for Sasha on June 28th. True to form, Sasha deposited a fresh poop sample in the waiting room. Dr. Dawn was not in yet so fortunately there was no howling on this morning.

Elizabeth retrieved Sasha from my arms and was frowning as she said,

"What's wrong with our little angel girl? You don't look so good missy."

Sasha managed to wag her tail a bit so Elizabeth grinned and said,

"Ooh, much better now." as she took her back to for procedure preparation.

The receptionist explained Dr. Dawn would call me later that day after reviewing the test results. I went to work but was anxious the whole time. I was self-employed at this time and worked alone which left me with no one to distract me from my own thoughts. I put on my iPod and worked with no drive or focus waiting for the phone to ring.

Sasha, Extraordinary Dachshund

CJ & Sasha together, 2007

Losing Sasha

Dr. Dawn phoned me around 2:00 that afternoon with the bad news. I listened to her explain the ultra sound showed severely cystic bilateral kidneys, enlarged adrenal glands, liver and spleen, and a huge gall bladder suggestive of a tumor.

After hearing all this all I could ask was, "Is Sasha in pain?"

Dr. Dawn responded, "Very much so."

I asked, "Is there any medication you could prescribe to ease her suffering?"

She replied, "Yes, I can make her comfortable for a short while but I want you to come in to see me as my last appointment this afternoon."

"I'll be there," I said.

Dr. Dawn said, "CJ, I have dreaded this conversation for years which is why I want you to come in. Think about euthanasia before you get here. Sasha is suffering and I know you cannot bear that. As I promised you years ago, I will be here for you. Have Mel drive you, OK?"

I immediately called Mel to give him the grim news. I was incapable of working any more that day. All I wanted was to get to Sasha and hold her. I sobbed during the whole 20-minute drive home. My heart and mind wrestled while I cried. Picture these two formidable opponents in a wrestling match:

In the red corner - my heart fighting for my selfish side and wanting to hold onto Sasha no matter what;

In the blue corner - my mind fighting on Sasha's behalf, asking for compassion and an unselfish love.

My heart was crumbling as my brain processed flashbacks of my life with Sasha. I felt like my body would just fall apart. My emotions rapidly changed between laughter and sorrow. I argued with myself in the car.

My blue corner mind was screaming to my heart, "This is not about you!"

Then more gently stating, "Think about Sasha, her pain – not yours."

My red corner heart jumped in saying, "I'll cowgirl up for you. Together we'll get through this. Maybe she'll be just fine."

It happened that Mel was driving in front of me as we had been working on the same side of town. We arrived at our home at the same time and he immediately came over to hold me as I got out of the car. Mel said,

"I couldn't stand looking in my rear view mirror and seeing you in so much pain. I almost rear-ended a car in front of me, as I couldn't take my eyes off you! At each stoplight I wanted to get out of the van to come back and hold you."

He knew this was just about the worst kind of sorrow I could possibly feel. Mel understood that even though I had those selfish feelings I would never allow Sasha to suffer. Mel understood I was letting Sasha go and that I needed to have my emotional time before I saw her.

It took about two hours before I could pull myself together enough to get in the car for the trip to Broadway Veterinary Hospital. I cried softly all the way there but knew I had to be positive and strong for Sasha. We arrived about 4:30 to be greeted by some of the staff, which had treated Sasha for years. They seemed emotional knowing what I might have to do. They brought Sasha out immediately and sent our little family into a private room just to be with her. (It's been two years now and I am sobbing while writing this part, I'm sure all pet lovers understand that.)

Sasha was so beautiful and happy to see us but we could tell she was in extreme pain. Maybe that was my imagination because she didn't seem in so much pain when I left her earlier that day. Or maybe now, my rose colored glasses were off and I could see the truth.

I don't know for sure. I did my best not to cry while holding Sasha but my heart was shattered so Mel took her from my arms. Dr. Dawn joined us in the private room and we discussed the ultra sound results at length. Dr. Dawn even lost some of her composure while going over the results. The three of us decided euthanasia was best for Sasha.

A long time ago, walking up to the hospital entrance for an appointment with Sasha, I witnessed a burly biker-type dude exit the hospital carrying his euthanized black lab. I doubt seriously this man cried in public, as he was a real tough-guy type. I may have been the only one to see that tear roll down his face. This tough guy seemed oblivious to my presence as we passed each other in the parking lot. This encounter affected me so dramatically that I immediately told Dr. Dawn I would be incapable of walking with Sasha, dead in my arms. She promised that if and when the time came she would euthanize Sasha at our home for me.

And even though I handled myself so well when she euthanized Squirt, Dr. Dawn offered to drive over to our home to euthanize Sasha because she wanted to spare me as much pain as possible. I declined her kind thoughtful offer, mainly because Mel was with me and could handle Sasha's body for me if I lost my composure.

Dr. Dawn left us to be alone with Sasha, and Mel and I took turns holding her. Mel was holding it together but I could tell he was deeply affected by this situation. Between the impending loss of Sasha and feeling my pain and sorrow, Mel's heart was also breaking.

Dr. Dawn came back in to administer a sedative for Sasha. I held Sasha next to my heart the whole time. She was warm and smelled sweet. She snuggled up with her head on my shoulder as Mel held us both. We waited about ten minutes for the sedative to take effect and Sasha relaxed in my arms while Mel stroked her. Mel softly said his goodbyes to Sasha, as he did not want to be in the room when Dr. Dawn administered the drugs. I suggested he go across the street to get some beer.

After Mel left, Dr. Dawn came in with an assistant to administer the euthanasia drug. Both of them were tearing up. We talked to Sasha and lovingly stroked her saying our goodbyes and telling her what a good girl she had always been. Sasha did not want to go, and fought the drug with everything she had. It was heart wrenching for the three of us and Dr. Dawn was amazed how Sasha fought off the drug. She requested another dose be prepared immediately, the whole time comforting me and Sasha while fighting off her own emotions. The technician rushed back in with another syringe and Dr. Dawn injected Sasha again while lovingly apologizing to her.

Sasha took her last breath looking into my loving face. This gave me peace as her last vision was of me loving her. She was so beautiful and had a look of serenity that I couldn't understand but wasn't surprised by. Dr. Dawn had to leave the room and the assistant went to make up a cardboard casket with a special blanket for Sasha, just like they did for Squirt. I was alone with Sasha, at peace and pain-free in my arms. At that very moment I felt I made the correct choice for Sasha. I also knew that I would never recover from this grief. I thanked God for letting me have this angel in my life for 14 years.

By the time Mel returned with the 12-pack of Bud Light we had placed Sasha in the coffin. Mel could not open the lid. He did not want to see Sasha that way.

Dr. Dawn came back in and said,

"That's it, I'm done for the day as this affected me more than most do."

Mel tossed Dr. Dawn and me a beer and as we were opening ours he took one for himself. I looked at him with surprise and he said,

"At a time like this even I want a drink."

Considering that Mel didn't like beer I knew this was just another symptom of his grief process. We toasted Sasha then sat there for about 45 minutes telling Sasha stories.

Dr. Dawn had been Sasha's vet from the beginning of her life. Throughout that time she had always commented on what an extraordinary dachshund Sasha was, which is how this book got its title.

We took our baby, Sasha, home and buried her in our back yard. We marked her grave with a metal dachshund sculpture I had had for some time. My best friend, Mary, found a flat river stone and painted "Sasha" on it to set above the grave. Every day I see the markers, one of the stories I've told you in this book comes to mind.

Mom cried with me as I told her every detail of that horrific day on the telephone. She felt my pain and understood my grief at the loss of my baby. When I called my Dad to let him know I had to euthanize Sasha he was genuinely upset for me. I know I reside in the softest section of his heart and with words of compassion, even though he was 2000 miles away, daddy wiped away his little girl's tears.

It took a while to get used to Sasha being gone. For months we still sat our plates on the floor after finishing a meal. I still have to consciously eat the last bite of my ice cream. Sasha always got the last bite or lick.

Sasha, Extraordinary Dachshund

CJ Adams

"No matter how little money and few possessions you own, having a dog makes you rich."

Louis Sabin

Financial Stuff

We lovingly referred to Sasha as our $15,000.00 dachshund but if truth were told I am sure we spent much more than that on her care. Please understand, I would have spent whatever was necessary for Sasha's health and well-being. All devoted animal lovers understand this. The only expense that ever surprised me was the root canal in 1999. FYI, it is just as expensive to root canal a dog's tooth as it is a human's. Under normal circumstances I would have elected to have the tooth extracted but dachshunds have large back molars and extracting them would be equal to removing two – three molars in other dogs. Dr. Dawn referred us back to Mountain View Animal Clinic as they had a canine dental specialist, Dr. Hawkins. The procedure was done in one appointment even though Dr. Hawkins had to deal with multiple roots and Sasha handled it like the trooper that she was.

Sasha, Extraordinary Dachshund

Even though we were faithful in having both Sasha's and Squirt's teeth cleaned yearly and sometimes bi-annually they still required some extractions throughout their lives. Gum disease in our animals is just as devastating to their health as it is to ours and small dogs need their teeth cleaned at least once a year. I always felt we were charged fair prices for services rendered by all professionals involved with the well-being of our animals. It wasn't like we had money to spare, it was just necessary and somehow we'd make it fit into our budget.

One of my mother's favorite stories to tell is of the time we had to take her Pomeranian, Sadie, to her veterinarian, Dr. Bob Stewart of Oakridge Animal Clinic in Oakridge, Oregon. Oakridge is such a small town that Oakridge Animal Clinic is only open on Wednesdays. You don't make an appointment; you just show up and wait your turn. I left Sasha and Mel at Mom's place while I went with her for company. There were two patients ahead of us and while waiting for our turn it was a pleasure to watch the tech/receptionist, Rayetta Clark, and Dr. Stewart interact with the animals and humans. Everyone knows everyone and their animals and I felt right at home in this environment. Mom wanted to have Dr. Stewart look at Sadie because she was limping a bit and I had hit the panic button just knowing Sadie was going to be paralyzed as Sasha had been.

Mom and I were both in the room while Dr. Stewart examined Sadie, making small talk and she laughingly mentioned my fear of Sadie's imminent paralysis. He responded that Sadie was in no danger of paralysis and that she was suffering a mild form of hip dysplasia that is common among the Pomeranian breed. Dr.

Stewart explained he could do surgery at his Eugene Clinic but that it was expensive and not necessary at this point. I boldly asked him if acupuncture would be effective and his face went blank as he pondered if I was serious or not. Mom assured him I was serious and went on to explain how we treated Sasha and had nicknamed her "The $15,000.00 Dachshund." Smiling, Dr. Stewart looked at me and said,

"Lady you live in the wrong town. You should live here where we believe it is our job to make your pet more valuable!"

This Oakridge office was small and very primitive compared to Broadway Veterinary Hospital. Dr. Stewart weighed Sadie by first standing on a regular scale to get his own weight then picked up Sadie and weighed again with her in his arms. I about fell over in laughter and definitely fell in love with his establishment. I also felt like Dr. Stewart connected to both pets and their owners. Mom and I were very comfortable and most importantly, so was Sadie. While leaving the clinic I told Mom, "I'd gladly bring Sasha here for treatment any day."

Dr. Stewart also practices at Delta Oaks Veterinary Clinic, a larger practice in Eugene, Oregon that is about 40 miles from Oakridge. When Mom informed me of this other, more modern clinic I was even more impressed he would devote one full day a week to the pets residing in Oakridge.

In recommending alternative treatments to other pet owners I always start by telling them to first examine what their animal is worth to them then examine what can be gained by additional treatment and therapy. I know I am not the "norm" but neither was Sasha. Most people we know, even animal lovers, think we took extraordinary measures for Sasha's paralysis and I always respond to those comments that Sasha was an extraordinary dachshund. The one thing I know for sure is that Sasha was worth every penny we spent on her. She was only four when paralyzed and she lived to be fourteen. The alternative treatments gave me ten more good years.

Knowing everything I know today, I would do it all over again – even more. If it had been physically possible and Squirt was a younger dog I would have taken him to Seattle for an operation to stop his tumor from bleeding out. It just wasn't practical to put such a mature pet in that situation. Sasha's final maladies were age related and I may have been able to get another six months with her if we aggressively treated her symptoms but those six months would have been just for me. I knew it was selfish of me to want more time so I gave Sasha my ultimate love by letting her go.

My heart breaks each time I recall the decisions I made to euthanize both Squirt and Sasha. I know I did the right thing for them but I still have to convince my heart it was the right thing for me too. To this day my heart hurts from missing them so much. I know there was no time left for Squirt as his tumor was bleeding out so I am at peace with that decision. However I sometimes wonder if I could have had a few more months with Sasha. Was she telling me she wasn't ready to leave me when she resisted the first euthanasia shot? Did I miss a special moment? I'll never know why Sasha resisted but it was definitely in her character. I know we couldn't stop the process, as she would have died within the hour from the first shot. I dream of them often and sometimes awake from sleep thinking they are still with me, especially Sasha.

Sasha, Extraordinary Dachshund

CJ Adams

"If there are no dogs in heaven, then when I die I want to go where they went."

Will Rogers

Grief

One sunny afternoon I took Sasha to Broadway Veterinary Hospital for a check-up. Sasha and I were excited to see Dr. Dawn and share some time with fellow animal lovers. As we were walking through the parking lot toward the back door entrance I saw this tall, dark haired man coming out carrying a very big black Labrador retriever. He walked out standing tall carrying this dog hanging over his arms that were sticking out at 90-degree angles, The man was staring

181

straight ahead. The black lab's eyes were open and his tongue was hanging out so I thought it was still anesthetized from a procedure so in passing I said,

"Tough day, huh?"

This man was not aware Sasha and I existed and we were right in front of each other when I spoke. As he passed by I noticed tears streaming down his face. I paused, expecting him to reply. He never broke stride and or even acknowledged me. It hit me then - that dog must be dead! Oh my God, he was carrying his dead pet home and could care less about anything else. Uncharacteristically Sasha just sat down, she didn't even approach this man for attention. Feeling his pain and sorry for what I had said, I turned to watch him.

I observed him carefully shift the limp body of his black lab to one shoulder and reach into his blue jean pocket for keys. He fumbled to get them into the lock of the camper shell covering his green full size pick-up truck. He managed to get the key in, twist the lever to release the latch and raise the door. He then lowered the truck's tailgate, put the dog on that tailgate then pulled out a blanket. He spread the blanket out, put the dog on it and sobbed as he carefully wrapped the edges around his beloved dog. He gently pushed the blanketed pet into the bed of the truck, closed the tailgate and lowered the camper shell door. He then turned around, leaned back against the truck as he bent over and threw up.

After wiping his mouth with the arm sleeve of his jacket he patted the camper shell twice with a flat hand and walked head down and slumped shoulders to get into the driver's side door. With Sasha on her leash I had been standing about fifteen feet away from him the entire time. Trust me, he had no idea I was there. He sat in the truck for a moment before starting the engine and leaving the parking lot to bury his beloved friend. It was truly a tough day for him!

This was the only time I ever witnessed Sasha enter Broadway Veterinary Hospital with a lowered and non-wagging tail. If I had a tail, I wouldn't have been able to wag it either.

About five months after losing Sasha Mel and I had to pick up keys to a rental property to perform maintenance in preparation for a new tenant. Dorothy Hardee, the property manager, had a home office so we stopped there to get the keys and to discuss the details of what repairs were necessary. Even though we had worked for Hardee Property Management this was the first time I met Dorothy in person. We arrived to find her home gloriously decorated for the Christmas Holidays. We were unaware she had a dachshund but I caught a flash of this little creature as it darted across the second story landing. Interrupting Dorothy and Mel's conversation I asked what her name was. Dorothy replied, "Sadie."

Naturally I had to pet her so I began calling her name as I worked my way up the stairway in the foyer. I lost all focus on why we were there and I was doing my best to entice this cutie toward me. Dorothy was telling us all about Sadie and how sweet and loving she was. After a minute or so of prancing back and forth on the landing Sadie finally came down the stairway to me. I picked her up and took in her scent and it was glorious. This was the first time I had held another animal since losing Sasha. Sadie was all wiggly and loving and started licking my face.

I was suddenly overcome with emotion and began crying softly as I snuggled Sadie close to my heart. Dorothy and Mel were discussing work details as my soft crying quickly turned into a meltdown. Dorothy was horrified as she thought my crying was due to Sadie biting me. She started stammering as she explained to Mel that Sadie had never bitten anyone. Coming up the stairs to check me out she was apologizing so I put Sadie down to show her I had not been bitten.

My crying turned to sobbing as Dorothy's husband John came out of the kitchen to see what all the fuss was about. I could no longer control myself as five months of dealing with Sasha's loss poured out of me. I crumpled down onto the stairs and just let it out as Mel explained my grief to Dorothy and John. Now Dorothy began to cry. Sadie went back upstairs to a blanket on her warm bed and John went back toward the kitchen as neither of them cared for all this crying.

I was thoroughly embarrassed by my display of emotion but after a few minutes I managed to gain some composure and apologized to Dorothy for my unprofessional behavior. While still crying, Dorothy graciously explained there was no need for me to be embarrassed and then told us her about her own incident. She experienced an unexpected emotional display a few months after the death of her father. Dorothy was showing a property when she was overcome with grief and had her own meltdown in front of perfect strangers at a time when she needed to be her most professional.

We hugged and cried some more but I felt relieved that she understood my grief and didn't judge me harshly for it. This shared emotion and the fact she had a dachshund endeared her to me and started our friendship.

After my meltdown at Dorothy's I felt strong enough to hold other animals so I decided to visit our Humane Society just to give the animals some love and myself a 'fix'. On my first visit I got emotional and cried as I walked around the cages speaking to the dogs. During this visit a darling little girl was walking around with her Mom and Dad looking for a dog to adopt when she saw me on the other side of a row of cages. This little girl came around to where I was standing, looked up and said,

"Don't worry, I'm sure you'll find your dog. When did you lose it? What kind of dog was it? Maybe we saw it in here somewhere!"

She turned to her parents, who were following her around the cages and asked,

"Can I help her find it?"

She had to be about twelve years old and wanted to help me look through all the cages for my lost dog. When I explained I wasn't looking for a lost dog but that I was there to just give the dogs some loving she asked me,

"Why are you crying then? Can't you find one you want?"

I replied, "My problem is I want them all and that is why I am crying."

She said, "You don't have to cry because we will help you to choose one. What kind do you want?"

While her parents watched and listened I took a moment to explain why I was there visiting the stray dogs. I think the girl understood me, but it broke my heart to tell her because she was there looking for a new pet. I was there grieving for my losses and I felt bad for subjecting this girl to my grief. I've never been back.

I will have another dachshund one day and I look forward to that time. We currently have Mom's cat, Hope. It took Hope a while to forgive us for all those years Sasha terrorized her but she has settled into our home quite nicely and I do so enjoy the comfort she provides. I think pet lovers deserve an extraordinary animal, at least once in their life and I hope all of you have been so blessed. I tried to live without an animal and was just not a happy person. My Mom once told me that love is worth the heartbreak. I now know my heart needs to love animals, as it somehow completes me. I can only explain that it is just how God made me.

CJ Adams

Why Write This Memoir?

In February 2009 I started dreaming about Sasha nightly. This was unusual, as I hadn't really dreamed of her for the past 20 months. I would wake up very upset that my dream was over. I felt like I had Sasha back and I wanted to hold onto that feeling and keep it to myself. However, it seemed to me that Sasha wanted me to write her story. I know that sounds weird but I don't know how to explain it better than that. Once I had decided I would write her story the dreams ended and I set out on this journey. I've marveled, laughed and cried my way through this memoir and I can only hope you did the same.

It is now October, 2011 and I want to add this additional explanation as to why I decided to publish this memoir. I was driving downtown Boise back in July and saw a lady walking a dachshund whose hind-end was in a wheeled cart. I had to find a place to pull over as I began crying. I decided then and there that I had to publish this memoir. I have to let pet owners know that there are alternative treatments. If one

187

Sasha, Extraordinary Dachshund

person becomes aware of and seeks out additional treatment – whether traditional or holistic - for their own extraordinary pet because of reading this book then they may be as blessed as I was with having Sasha in my life.

Thank You

I want to thank the following people, who were extraordinary in their own ways and worked with me in writing this memoir:

My Mel – for his infinite patience. He is my heart, soul and one true love.

My family – for they always accepted and loved me, and still do.

Dr. Dawn Sessions – a Goddess of a person, an extraordinary veterinarian and the first one to mention to me there were other options available in treating Sasha. Dr. Sessions practices veterinary medicine, along with her incredible staff, at Broadway Veterinary Hospital, 350 East Linden Ave., Boise, ID 83706 208-344-5592.

Dr. Debra Mack – the one who believed she could, and then did, heal my Sasha. Dr. Mack is the reason I had a story to write. I am grateful she took the time to look up Sasha's 9-year-old records and to contribute to this story. Dr. Mack did read and edit the section about her treatments of Sasha so that I could accurately pass on to you how Sasha was healed.

Dr. Jacquie Allgire – who also took the time to find Squirt's and Sasha's records in a storage facility. Dr. Jacquie Allgire is practicing holistic veterinary medicine in Phoenix, Arizona at Alta Vista Veterinary Hospital.

Dr. Patricia Saras, DVM – for taking time out of her busy schedule to be interviewed for the Holistic Veterinary Medicine chapter of this book. Dr. Saras owns and practices holistic veterinary medicine at Animal Healing Center, Integrative Veterinary Medicine 5500 W. Emerald St., Boise, ID 83706 208-424-7755

Dr. Rebecca Paulekas, DVM, MPT for her valuable knowledge and insight into the Holistic Veterinary Medicine. Dr. Paulekas is practicing at WestVet Animal Emergency and Specialty Center, 5018 N. Sawyer Ave, Garden City, Idaho 83714 208-375-1600

Amber Youngman – my beloved niece, who, with her keen eye and intelligent mind, proofread the initial drafts.

Diane Evans - as she was the first person who told me I had the talent to write a book.

Susan Ernest, Janet Young , CJ Ensign and Jayne Black – for their honest opinions, advice and keen eyes.

Laura and Bruce Delaney, owners of my favorite store, "Rediscovered Bookshop" and their marvelous staff, Ross, Wally, Whitney and Ty. They are all truly "my people."

Elaine Ambrose, an author and a publisher but also my writing mentor and a very sassy friend. Her advice, encouragement and handholding helped me to write this memoir.

About the Author

I wrote this memoir to let all animal guardians know there are many healing options available for your treasured pets. In the process I began to heal from the loss of Sasha and now will begin a search for my next little friend. I am grateful you honored Sasha and me by reading our story. Still happily married to Mel, I live in Boise, Idaho.

Visit our website at dachsielove.com. You may contact CJ at cj@dachsielove.com